T
ANTIQUE

The Handbook of
ANTIQUE FURNITURE

Plantagenet Somerset Fry

BARRIE & JENKINS

LONDON

A la Gloire du Chêne

First published in Great Britain in 1992
by Barrie & Jenkins Ltd., Random Century House,
20 Vauxhall Bridge Road, London SW1V 2SA

A catalogue record for this book is available from the
British Library

ISBN 0 7126 5460 7

Illustrations by David Dawson

Designed by Roger Walker

Typeset by Edna A. Moore, ☛ Tek-Art, Addiscombe,
Croydon, Surrey

Printed in England by Clays Ltd, St Ives, plc

Contents

Appendices

Introduction

This is a guide to furniture styles of the world – not the whole world and not all the styles, but a representative selection of what are considered to be the most important. It is not an attempt to trace the development of furniture, whatever that may mean. I do not believe furniture necessarily develops or improves in function or quality of style. Some of today's furniture is excruciatingly uncomfortable to sit or lie on, or work at, or hideously ugly to look at, whereas some Louis XV armchairs were – and still are – beautiful to behold and almost luxurious to sit in. It is rather an essay of historical exploration round the houses and museums of the world, stopping off here and there in different periods to see what was being made and used as furniture.

There are many terms used in identifying pieces of furniture, but in the end it all boils down to a basic five pieces: things to sit on, to lie on, to eat, work, write and play at, to put things away in and take out again when needed, and to use for display purposes; in other words, chairs, stools, settees, benches; beds and couches; tables and desks; chests and cupboards; shelves. These are the ingredients of this book, and things like lampstands, clocks, looking glasses and screens are for the most part omitted.

The question is frequently asked, When is furniture properly considered to be antique? There have long been two qualifications. For Inland Revenue or H M Customs purposes in Britain, furniture is antique if it is over one hundred years old. The furniture dealing establishment, however, generally stipulates 130 or more years old. Abroad, different criteria apply. Because there are these two alternative criteria in Britain, I have thought it appropriate to take the one hundred year plus figure and I have therefore included some Art Nouveau.

The guide is arranged as follows: the main text covers Africa and the Near East, the Far East, Europe, and the Americas, in that order. There are appendices outlining the emergence of Art Nouveau, explaining the system of stamping of names of cabinet-makers on furniture made in Paris in the eighteenth century, and listing the principal public collections in the world where readers can see examples of the styles of furniture mentioned in the text. There is a glossary of terms used in furniture, principally those found in the main text, and there is a list of some of the works consulted in the preparation of the book, which readers may take up for further study.

The line drawings have been done and most of the photographs have been taken by my friend and neighbour David Dawson, artist, teacher and photographer, a singularly appropriate combination of skills to draw upon to illustrate this work, and I am greatly indebted to him. I am grateful

7

also to Keith Bycroft for casting his expert eye over the text and making several very valuable suggestions which I took up. I have also had much good help from Andrew Singleton, Thane Meldrum, Peter Foster, Sara Muldoon, and Edward and Eva Johnson. Publishers seldom get thanked by authors, and I am very pleased to acknowledge my gratitude to Messrs Barrie & Jenkins, particularly to Euan Cameron and Mary Scott.

Plantagenet Somerset Fry

Africa and the Near East

(1) ANCIENT EGYPT

Throughout a long history of at least 2500 years, ancient Egyptian furniture was on the whole simple in design and mainly functional. Some pieces, such as thrones, made specially for pharaohs, were more elaborate and often heavily jewelled. But the bed made for Hetepheres (below), mother of pharaoh Cheops, c.2600BC, could have been made for anyone entitled to have one and who could afford it. When pharaoh Tutankhamun's tomb (fourteenth century BC) was discovered and opened by Howard Carter and the Earl of Carnarvon in 1922, a great variety of furniture was found in the ante-chamber, heaped up as if in some sort of Egyptian equivalent of an auctioneer's warehouse. Some pieces were ornate and jewelled, others were in simple styles. One elaborate piece was Tutankhamun's throne which was overlaid in gold, coloured glass and semi-precious stones.

Ancient Egyptians believed in an after-life, especially a pharaoh's. But he could only enjoy this if his body was properly buried, by embalming over a process lasting several weeks, and placing it in a tomb which was hermetically sealed. The earliest tombs were called *mastabas*. These were followed in the years c.2700 to c.2200, the period of the Old Kingdom dynasties, by pyramids, and later still, pharaohs of the New Kingdom were interred, after embalming, in huge rock tombs, like some of those at Abu Simbel, further south on the Nile, near the Second Cataract.

Because the pharaoh's body was preserved to make it easier for the soul to pass on to the after-life, it was also thought that the pharaoh would need to take with him those comforts he had enjoyed in his earthly life. Pharaohs' bodies were surrounded, whether in a stone sarcophagus or a mummy case, by a collection

The bed of Hetepheres, mother of pharaoh Cheops, c.2600 BC. (reconstructed from remains.)

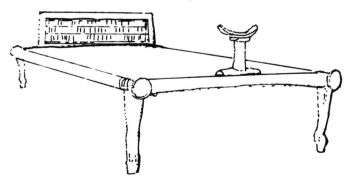

of precious jewels, weapons, household utensils, food and other paraphernalia, among which were pieces of furniture, not only those used by the pharaoh himself but also some belonging to his family or servants. The effective means by which some Egyptian tomb-sealing was carried out has enabled us in the present century, thousands of years later, to see some pieces in very good condition. Some of the wood and the leather upholstery appear to be in as good a state as they were when first put into the tombs.

These pieces, together with many others surviving from ancient Egypt, are among the oldest pieces of furniture in the world. They date at the earliest from about 2600BC. It is very interesting that the types of furniture and the manner in which they were made changed little between the 2600s and the years of the New Kingdom, which began in the sixteenth century BC.

Because strong wood was scarce in ancient Egypt, craftsmen had to import timbers like cedarwood, sycamore, olivewood and gopher (a kind of camphorwood which Noah used to make the Ark [Genesis 6, v 14]) from Lebanon and Palestine. They also obtained ebony and ivory from districts in the African interior south of Egypt. Egyptian craftsmen had at their disposal a variety of tools such as bronze saws, chisels, wooden mallets, metal axes and sharp knives. Although the plane had not yet been invented, surface shaping and finishing could be done well using an adze. Craftsmen also developed furniture-making techniques that have lasted with modifications ever since. They knew how to make mortise and tenon joints and to dovetail, and they had strong and durable glues. They produced bronze hinges for chest furniture and knew how to upholster chairs, stools and beds, using leather strap, plant fibres and cloth.

Upright chair inlaid with ebony and ivory. New Kingdom, Egypt, (c.1567–c.950 BC)

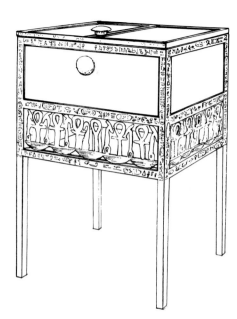

*Box on legs from
Tutankhamun's tomb,
mid-14th cent. BC*

The basic pieces of Egyptian furniture were chairs (thrones, and others) beds, boxes, chests and stools. The Egyptian chair often had a square seat on four carved wood animal legs that all faced forwards, and with a carved sloping back supported by upright stiles. The seat was often made of closely platted leather strapwork, or of rushes beaten into strong fibrous strips, nailed to the frame.

One widely used item appeared in the Middle Kingdom period (c.2040–1633BC) and this was the folding stool. Its seat consisted of a row of straps nailed or glued from rail to rail, or a removable square of leather stitched so as to fit over the corners of the frame. The stool legs terminated in carved ducks' beaks inlaid with ivory. This kind of stool was used not only domestically but also by commanders in the battlefield.

The Egyptians were among the first people to use the bed, and may have got the idea from the Saharan Africans. A number of examples have survived, some in good condition. The bed of Hetepheres is typical of a style that lasted for many centuries. Like some Egyptian chairs, the animal legs of some beds all faced forwards. What appears to be a headboard is actually a footboard. The sleeper rested his head on the wooden headrest which was a detachable part of the bed, and certainly looks uncomfortable. In the case of the Hetepheres bed, some of the woodwork had been encased in gold leaf, and the bedframe was upholstered with a lattice of leather strapping or plant fibre.

Among the treasures found in Tutankhamun's tomb were boxes, caskets, and chests, containing things like linen, toys, paints and jewels. Some caskets were partitioned inside, like Victorian work- or writing-boxes, and some had domed lids. One chest was mounted on four square legs, with a hinged lid, the box part being edged with a decoration of hieroglyphics.

(2) ASSYRIA AND PERSIA

Unlike Egypt, the ancient empires of Assyria and Persia have left no tangible evidence of their furniture. We know something from sculptured tableaux on stone panels which have emerged in the last two hundred years of excavations in the Near East, chiefly on the sites of royal palaces, such as that of Sennacherib, emperor of Assyria in the seventh century BC. What has been found is largely associated with imperial or religious ceremonial, with warfare, or with everyday life in the courts of ancient despots.

8th cent. BC stone relief showing Assyrian emperor and his wife at dinner. He is reclining on a couch, she sits on a high chair with a footstool, and before them is a table. Note inverted cone feet.

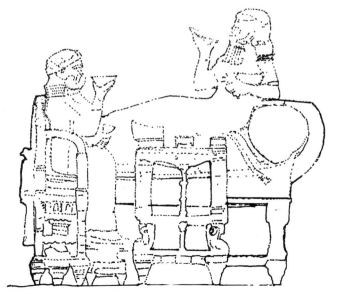

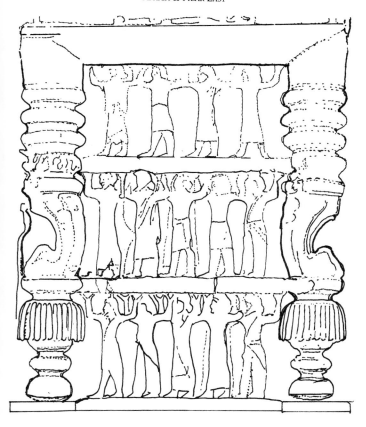

6th cent. BC Persian stone relief illustrating the seat part of a Persian throne.

Assyrian emperors sat on thrones constructed so as to raise them above the level of those in their company. These seem to have been high-backed and straight, and the emperor's elevated position was emphasized by the need for a footstool to get on to it and to rest his feet when there. Though the pictorial evidence of these thrones usually related to rulers, it is clear that emperors' wives, and perhaps in some cases their sons, as well as high priests, also used throne-like chairs. The table on page 12 has straight legs that have animal paws near the bottom and then end in inverted cones as feet. Other sculptured reliefs show chairs having animal feet, such as lions' paws or horses' hooves. These inverted cones are also

13

found on portrayals of beds, couches and tables. An interesting stone relief from the palace of Sennacherib shows a troop of armed men carrying a number of pieces of furniture along the tow-path of a river. One piece is a round table on three legs which intersect half way down to form a short tripod base.

Ancient Persian furniture was much the same as Assyrian furniture, which may be because the Persians took over the lands of the Assyrians and absorbed their art forms and building techniques. The ancient capital city of Persepolis, about 40 miles north-east of modern Shiraz, was founded by Darius I, king of Persia from c.520 to 486BC. Stone reliefs found in the ruins during excavations illustrate something of imperial furniture. The range of items is somewhat limited, though there are a number of throne-like chairs. The figure on page 13 shows the lower part of a Persian throne of the period and the incorporation of animal paws in the chair's legs seen in Assyrian thrones is repeated, though somewhat further up the leg. The legs themselves are interesting in that they are in part turned, with disc and inverted cup motifs. It is probable that wood-turning techniques originated in ancient Persia, executed with a primitive pole lathe. Turning as a decorative treatment has continued round the world ever since, though not in China where the turned effect was always produced by other means.

(3) ISLAMIC FURNITURE: FIFTEENTH TO NINETEENTH CENTURIES

There has been nothing like the variety of furniture made or used in the Islamic world as there has been in Europe, the Far East or the Americas. The domestic habits of Muslims have been very different. They were accustomed to sitting on rugs on the floor for meals, holding meetings and in company generally. Sometimes they sat or lay beside low tables, on divans or low couches. For the most part, Muslims lived in warm climates and spent much of their day out of doors, in court-yards or gardens. Even their beds were close to the ground, either in the form of piles of rugs with additional cushions, or as divans. The divan, thought to have originated in Persia, was a bench-like structure, or a raised part of flooring, like a stage, along one wall of a room, which was covered with soft cushions, rugs and coverlets.

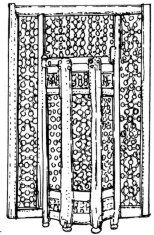

15th cent. AD Mamluk period Egyptian ivory and wood screen.

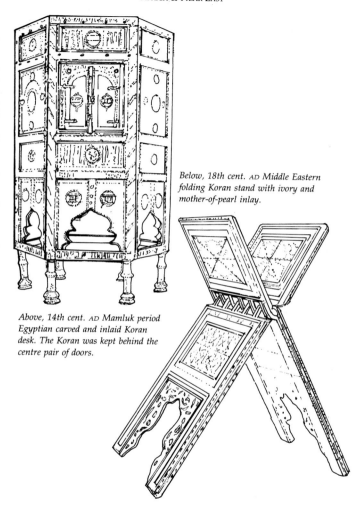

Below, 18th cent. AD Middle Eastern folding Koran stand with ivory and mother-of-pearl inlay.

Above, 14th cent. AD Mamluk period Egyptian carved and inlaid Koran desk. The Koran was kept behind the centre pair of doors.

Little or no decoration was applied to the framework. The colourful attractiveness of the Islamic bed lay in its coverings and soft furnishings.

In the period c.1450 to c.1700, some small tables, low stools and small cabinets were popular. Being easily portable, they could be moved about the house, for use in one part at one moment, and in another the next. They were often decorated with inlays of ivory and mother-of-pearl; some patterns were pictorial within the limits allowed by Islamic custom, but more usually the designs were geometrical, and these were often executed with wonderful skill and intricacy. Screens were also made, some with close-knit lattice patterns of wood, turned or square edged, within a frame.

Islamic decorative designs had great influence in many parts of Europe after about 1400. Between about 1400 and 1700, Venetian furniture decorators, for example, produced highly sophisticated geometric inlays of coloured bone and ebony, later called *certosina* work, after the Carthusian monks who adopted this intricate style.

Two pieces of furniture associated with Muslim religion and more usually made for use in mosques but which sometimes appeared in houses were Koran stands and Koran desks. The Koran stand was really the Muslim equivalent of the lectern, and was generally a simple X-shaped piece of furniture, with the articulating join between the two boards placed higher up than central (see page 15). These boards were the subject of fine decorative treatment, inlay, intarsia and carving, with latticework or other piercing, and with much use of ivory, mother-of-pearl and even metals such as tin. The Koran desk was a larger, more elaborate piece produced in a variety of shapes, but was basically intended as an imposing and finely crafted container in which to store the house copy of the Koran. Some desks look like small portable pulpits on short legs (and indeed, some were used in that capacity). Some have a fine domed top. In some types, the Koran itself was stored behind a pair of heavily decorated doors in the carcase.

The variety of Islamic furniture became a little more extensive in the eighteenth century. In Persia, for example, which had been enjoying a national revival of architecture, art and craft skills (notably in silverwork, ivory carving and faience and carpet-making), a number of small items of furniture already produced for rich clients now began to appear in greater quantities. To a variety of small inlaid tables (a polygonal plan was perhaps the most popular) were added ches's, writing boxes, small cabinets, jewel boxes with domed lid and fall front revealing *vargueño*-like rows of small drawers (see page 17), and of course screens. Preferred woods included sandalwood, ebony (especially the Macassar kind) and cedar. Craftsmen were experienced in lacquer-work, which was applied not only to wood but also to papier-mâché, especially boxes, trays and stools. Very little of this Persian furniture has survived but we know of its wide distribution and use from the large number of paintings produced by Persian artists which often portrayed contemporary domestic scenes and included the normally sparse furnishings. Sometime towards the close of the eighteenth century, European influences began to reach Persian painting, and after that it was not long before some furniture was made with European forms in mind.

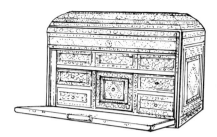

late 18th/early 19th cent. AD Persian jewel casket inlaid with ivory and stones, from Shiraz.

In India under Mughal rule (1526 to towards the end of the eighteenth century), almost the only furniture that has been investigated in depth is beds for rulers and princes, and their seat furniture, particularly thrones and chairs. Both categories were given much consideration. The bed, like European late mediaeval beds, served the dual role for sleeping at night and receiving people during the day. Mughal beds had highly decorated canopies, supported at the corners on four posts (see colour section). The canopy was either a simple, rectangular frame with colourful drapery, or a shaped canopy, like a gabled roof or even in the form of a dome, and more elaborately dressed. It is hard to say what the mattress was like, but ivory miniatures and polychrome paintings of the time show beds well provided with richly decorated cushions and bolsters. Beds stood on short feet, often bell-shaped. As for chairs, because it was customary to sit cross-legged, they were usually constructed wider and deeper than, say, European versions. Since chairs were meant principally for rulers, their wives, and, occasionally, senior court personnel, they were not made in great quantity.

(4) AFRICA: ELEVENTH TO NINETEENTH CENTURIES

The furniture of Africa has only recently been studied in any depth, but many museums and private collections of African arts and crafts have the most fascinating examples from West, East and South Africa, going back in numerous instances several hundred years. The range of pieces is small, confined mainly to beds, chairs, headrests, the relatively rare table, and the most important piece of all, the stool. But the variety of individual styles is enormous, and we can only touch on a small selection.

Most Africans slept on animal skins or on woven mats on the ground. The mat was an important possession, as it was used not only for sleeping but also for sitting on for meals and for discussion, and in some societies it was also a form of currency, used as a medium of exchange. The earliest mats of which traces have been found date back to the eighth century. Descriptions by

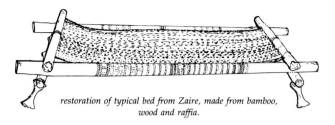

restoration of typical bed from Zaire, made from bamboo, wood and raffia.

Europeans of the sixteenth and seventeenth centuries draw attention to mats being woven from reeds, papyrus grass and bamboo, and point out that no African travelled without taking his rolled-up mat with him. Some mats were stretched across wooden frames supported on four Y-forks about one foot off the ground to make a bed. In Zaire, they had sheets and other bed linen. Many beds of this type were made broad enough for two. Some single beds were carved out of a single piece of wood, and examples have come from Nigeria and Cameroon.

Africans also had headrests, rather like those found in ancient Egyptian tombs, and it is now believed the Egyptians got the idea from the Saharan Africans, not *vice versa*. Some headrests were part of the bed, but more usually they were separate and portable. The basic design was two platforms separated by a short vertical post. The top platform was concave to support the neck, and the bottom platform completely flat. Many headrests had social or religious significance: a chief's head should not be allowed to touch the ground. Many headrests have survived, some, from Mali for example, going back to the twelfth and thirteenth centuries.

12th-14th cent. AD wooden head-rest from Mali. It is 7 ins from the middle of the head-piece to the ground.

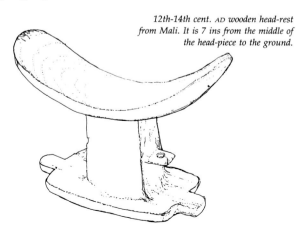

Chairs were relatively rare and very basic. Hardly more than an extension of a stool, they consisted mainly of a backrest with a seat, the whole being propped up on posts from behind. In some respects these chairs resembled the European backstool of the sixteenth and seventeenth centuries (see below), though many of the surviving examples are much older than that.

Like the mat, the stool was another important piece of furniture that most people carried with them, sometimes strapped to their backs. The earliest stools so far found date from the 800s, and come from Nigeria. They were generally of two basic kinds. One had a flat, solid top, oval, round, square, rectangular, or irregular shape, supported on three or four legs; the other was carved from a single piece of wood, and was usually cubical or cylindrical. The former was often made on the Ivory Coast, in Ghana and in Cameroon, the latter in Zaire and further east.

The stool was a very individual piece. Most were made locally by local woodcarvers. Some tribes believed that a stool housed the owner's soul, especially if it was a chief's, thus as it was passed

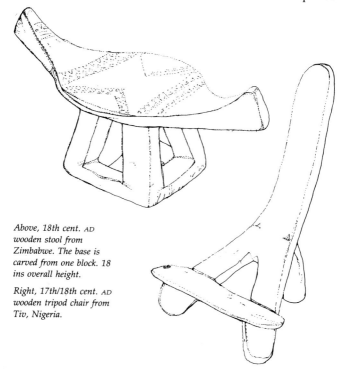

Above, 18th cent. AD wooden stool from Zimbabwe. The base is carved from one block. 18 ins overall height.

Right, 17th/18th cent. AD wooden tripod chair from Tiv, Nigeria.

19

down the generations, it became more and more sacrosanct. This was particularly the case with the Ashanti people in the eighteenth and nineteenth centuries (and to some extent still today). Their ruler was called the Asantehene. The first Asantehene had an elaborately made golden stool which looks like a headrest and is kept lying on its side. Its sanctity is such that it cannot be sat on under any circumstances, and is treated with great reverence. Stools were associated with leadership among many African peoples, including those of Uganda, Mali and Ghana.

A few African tables have survived from the great West African period of *c*.1000–*c*.1600. One kind was round topped with a carved bead-like edge to the rim, set on four stubby turned legs.

After the arrival of Europeans in Africa in the sixteenth century, some European furniture styles were copied by African craftsmen, particularly throne-like chairs, but they are not in the mainstream of traditional African furniture such as can be seen in many of the museums in North America that are listed in Appendix 3.

ASIA

CHINA, JAPAN AND SOUTH-EAST ASIA: THIRD CENTURY BC TO NINETEENTH CENTURY

Chinese Han dynasty (c.202 BC–c.220 AD) drawing of Li Ssu, chief adviser to the Ch'in emperor, Shih Huang-ti (221–210 BC).

The earliest furniture of ancient China, of which we have any helpful detail, is that in use during the Han dynasty (c.202BC to c.AD220). This information comes from contemporary clay models of Han houses, and pictures of house interiors. Something can also be deduced from Han period bronzes featuring domestic and religious artefacts. An early and central piece was the *k'ang*, which was an alcove platform bed, normally so large that it could also be used during the day as a withdrawing area with enough space for two or three people to recline beside low occasional tables. In the northern, colder areas, this bed arrangement was erected on a brick floor which had some form of underfloor-heating. Further south, the *k'ang* was a wooden structure incorporating both bed and tables on a timber platform. Later, upright and arm chairs were added as additional pieces of furniture, as well as stools, benches and screens, cupboards and chests. The oldest stool was a folding X type, not unlike the Roman *sella curulis* (see page 35) – and it is interesting to speculate which civilization got the idea from the other. To the Chinese, the X-shaped stool, and its partner, the X-shaped chair, were seats of honour for imperial and religious use.

There is a gap in our detailed knowledge of Chinese furniture from the AD 200s to the 620s, when the Tang dynasty (618–906) ruled. But from then on, through the Sung, Mongol, Ming and Manchu periods, down to the present century, there is an unbroken series of illustrations of one kind or another, giving a fascinating 'catalogue' of Chinese furniture. Perhaps the most interesting revelation from these pictures is that, on the whole, Chinese furniture styles hardly changed over nearly 2,000 years. And these styles were copied, with and without modification, in Japan, Korea, Thailand and Malaysia. The Japanese, for example, began to make folding X-shaped chairs and stools in the ninth century, initially as portable camp seats for the *samurai*.

Chinese furniture in these early times was produced in wood in the natural or the lacquered state, or it was made from bamboo (more usually in Southern China). Numerous woods were employed, often depending upon the locality of the workshops.

Late 15th/Early 16th cent. Chinese embroidered picture of a garden pavilion with a k'ang and an armchair (left).

Among the most readily identified were the hardwoods *hua-li-mu*, *huang-hua-li*, and *tzu-t'an*. All three are a little like rosewood, but the last-named, imported from the Philippine Islands, is also known in the West as purplewood. There was also *chi-ch'ih-mu*, or chicken wing wood, which was grey-brown, darkening to deep brown on waxing, and *chang-mu*, or camphorwood, which had a pleasant smell, and was particularly suitable for chests. In northern China, such woods were worked in the raw state and then waxed. Further south, woods were usually lacquered, to protect them against insects and to produce a surface that allowed relief carving and decoration. Chinese lacquerwork was brilliantly executed, using colours that included vermilion, red-brown, dark-green, black and gold.

Japanese furniture was made both from native woods and from woods imported from China, South East Asia and the Philippines, but for the most part the pieces were lacquered, and the range of items in the early centuries was small. Japanese lacquerwork had been developed in the eighth century and improved over the centuries. When the taste for lacquered wood furniture reached

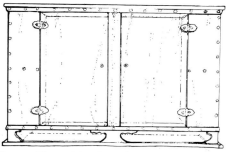

8th cent. Japanese Nara period cupboard of persimmon wood, with gilt copper mounts. 35 ins wide.

8th cent. Japanese Nara period low table, painted and part gilded. Height, about 4 ins. to lower edge of table top.

Europe in the second half of the seventeenth century, via pieces that came directly from Oriental makers, those produced in Japan were soon regarded as the finest. When English furniture makers, for example, began to make furniture in the raw and lacquer it *à la japonaise*, it was no coincidence that they coined the word 'japanning' to describe the lacquered finishes. Europeans never produced lacquerwork to the standard of the Chinese or Japanese. From about 1680 onwards, much Dutch and English furniture was therefore sent to the Far East to be lacquered in authentic Oriental style.

Two other features of Oriental furniture are of interest. Chinese chests, cupboards and some screens were fitted with metal mounts, lockplates, hinges and spandrels, and the metalwork was often countersunk to make it flush with the woodwork. Metal mounts go back many centuries, but the idea did not reach Europe until the seventeenth century where it was taken up widely and with great enthusiasm. Chinese furniture was also notable for the absence of dowels and nails for joints. The latter were usually produced by the mortise and tenon method, or by dovetailing, and there were a number of strong and durable glues. Joins were so well done that it was usually quite impossible to see them. Lacquered drawers were tailored to fit so exactly that the back was marked with a minute identifying 'chop', ensuring that every drawer was paired with its corresponding space.

Much Chinese furniture of the sixteenth and seventeenth centuries has survived, not only in China but also in Western and other museums and private collections, notably in London, Copenhagen, Paris, New York and Stockholm. Most of it is a continuation of older styles of Chinese furniture that reach back to such ancient times that they cannot be dated accurately. Some modifications were produced in this two-century span, which covers the last Ming emperors and the first Manchu emperors. The range includes chairs, cupboards, tables, chests and beds. Most of the pieces were lacquered, and other forms of decoration were inlays of stones and/or metal, ivory and contrasting woods, and sometimes stones.

Chinese chairs of the period were upright chairs, armchairs, folding chairs and throne-type chairs. Upright chairs often had solid seats, sometimes covered with wickerwork, on which a cushion was placed. The splat was generally a single central upright that curved in the middle and then straightened again, to

Below, 18th cent. Chinese red lacquered armchair. Below right, Early 17th cent. Chinese 'mandarin' chair in red lacquered wood and polychrome engraved decoration. Chair width, 47½ ins.

fit the sitter's back. Stretchers were fitted at low level, with a second row just below the seat. Some splats were decorated in gold and black lacquer. Seats of upright chairs were square or rectangular in plan, with straight legs, so that a number of chairs could be lined up together along a wall to make a bench or settle. Armchairs were more varied in design, many with the solid splat similar to the upright chair and with a similar solid seat, but arms could be slim and horizontal, with a latticework support below, or the back and arm supports could curve. A third type of armchair, more like a throne or small sofa, was usually very wide relative to its height; for example, 45 inches wide and 43 inches tall, with a seat up to 30 inches from front to back. The back might rise in steps to a high centre. The legs sometimes resembled elephants' trunks curved inward at the base, and an all-round stretcher frame was fitted under the feet, flush with the floor. One throne of this type from an imperial palace is decorated with cloisonné enamelwork of many colours. A variant on the throne chair was what is called a 'mandarin' chair (used by a top civil servant): some of these were lacquered in red with engraved polychrome decoration and a leg and stretcher motif similar to that of the throne-like armchairs.

Cupboards came in various styles, most with completely flat surfaces and rectilinear in design. They were invariably lacquered on front and sides, the two front doors having one picture over both surfaces and over the intervening upright stile between. Cupboards were made with one, two or even three pairs of doors. Some of the single pair of doors type had a compartment below the door level which was closed off on the front. One of two kinds of support was used, a separate base or short extensions of the corner stiles. The two, four or six-door cupboards were sometimes used in pairs side by side to create an extensive cupboard area, along a wall. The top – and usually smaller – pair of cupboard compartments were for hats, and the units were sometimes detachable. Most cupboards were also lacquered inside, especially on the reverse side of the doors, in colours that contrasted with those on the outside, and most cupboards were fitted with brass or other metal mounts and other applications.

Late 17th cent. Chinese lacquered cupboard with high relief decoration

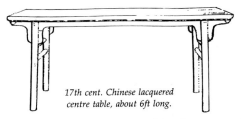

17th cent. Chinese lacquered centre table, about 6ft long.

Chinese tables of the period were of simple construction. They were either made in bamboo, when the legs were of course rounded, or heavy wood, when the legs were round or square. Some low tables, such as those made to accompany the other equipment of the *k'ang*, had cabriole legs, which were a Chinese invention, although the name is European. Dining tables were square or rectangular and only rarely round or oval. Their dimensions were such that a maximum of ten people could sit comfortably at them, because Chinese food is served in many dishes which all diners are expected to be able to reach from wherever they sit. Some dining tables were a few inches higher than the average Western kind, and this may be because the chairs used by the diners were high-seated and had a foot-bar or accompanying footstool. Table legs were generally vertical, but slightly slanted legs were fitted, perhaps for stability in a land subject to earthquakes. Tables were lacquered and sometimes had additional coloured ornamentation.

Sometime in the period there appeared the kneehole writing table, a later seventeenth-century type having two drawers flanking a central drawer over the kneehole. Another kind of table was what is sometimes called the 'melon' table, because of its shape. The table has a hexagonal top with six convex legs meeting a hexagonal frame at floor level. The top either consists of a slab of framed marble or is made of solid wood.

Chinese melon-shaped table with marble top, c.1650

Chests were used for storing clothes as well as books, manuscripts and treasured possessions. They were either flat-topped or domed, and were usually heavily lacquered. Some chests formed part of a two-chest set of the same horizontal dimensions, with the same metal mounts and the same or similar decoration. The lower chest, on short feet, might consist of a group of small drawers enclosed by a pair of doors.

Beds of the period followed the earlier styles, consisting of a fretwork or latticework canopy supported on four or six light posts, with a latticework frieze round the bed frame, broken at the front for access.

All these styles of furniture were constructed with concealed interlocking members. Decorative treatments other than the ubiquitous lacquerwork included bevelling of edges, sometimes convex, sometimes concave. Curves were invariably cut from a single piece of wood, and round posts, stretchers, legs and so on were always shaped by hand, never turned. Chinese craftsmen liked providing cane surfaces as decoration for hardwood backs or seats, and they also employed marble or other decorative stone in table tops, stools and other pieces. Longer table legs which were straight sometimes had hoof feet, sometimes turning inward. Extra strength for tables was provided by trellis-work aprons under the top.

Japanese furniture of the period was more limited in its range: most people slept on mats on the floor, many sat on them for meals served at very low tables. Much of what furniture the Japanese did use was either imported directly from China or modelled on Chinese styles, with modifications, particularly in the case of cabinets and small tables. The Japanese had built-in cupboards with sliding doors. There were some movable chests, and chests-on-chests. One interesting piece, not exclusively Japanese, as it was made in China and elsewhere in South East Asia, was the cabinet of three or four shelves, part open, part shut-off by small

16th cent. Japanese dome-lidded chest in black lacquer, with gold lacquer ornament and metal mounts.

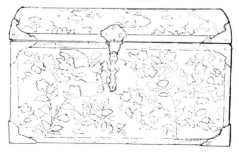

cupboard-type doors, with lacquer decoration and metal mounts, opening and shutting either on hinges or sliding from side to side. Today, this piece would perhaps be classed as a room divider, if of larger dimensions. The Japanese, however, had their own special room-divider, the screen, one of the most important and most widely used pieces of furniture, and one that frequently received the highest quality of artistic painting and decoration. These were meant not only to break up space in larger areas, but also to serve as draught excluders. Screens were two-, four-, six- and, rarely, eight-panelled, and some folded concertina-fashion. The wooden frames were light but strong, and the screen was made of tough paper. The paintings were generally different for each panel, the panels either making up a complete picture on the screen or a series of different pictures (one on each panel) whose themes might or might not be connected. Not all screens were of the concertina type: some were made so as to slide in special grooves along the floor. Another kind was the rolled up 'blind', or *sudare*, which, when let down, revealed a complete painting.

Another piece of Japanese furniture that continued to be made in some quantity was the folding stool, first copied from Chinese styles in the ninth century. The seventeenth-century Japanese kind was beautifuly decorated in lacquer and fitted with finely chased metal mounts. Some stools had a footstool on one of the footrails, and the seats were often of the finest coloured leather.

The furniture of eighteenth- and to a large extent nineteenth-century China varied little from ancient traditional styles which had served the Chinese so well for so long. Justice may be done to it by highlighting one or two new types of furniture introduced into the domestic and palatial range, and pointing to variations in decorative treatment. From about 1700, side and centre tables, ordinary and low-level, appeared as modifications of earlier versions. Some low-level tables had scroll legs, others had horse hoof feet on short, square legs. Screens, which had been made for many centuries, now appeared with as many as twelve folding panels, and were painted in bright colours, as well as the more usual black and gold. Chair furniture had already begun to be decorated in new, brighter colours, such as red-vermilion and brown, and this was now done on a wide scale.

16th cent. Japanese samurai folding stool in black lacquer, with gold lacquer ornament. The mounts are bronze.

In lacquer decoration of large surfaces like cabinet fronts, chests-on-chests, large boxes and so forth, designs incorporated exotic birds, rocks and more varied flowers.

The tambour sliding door for cupboards and cabinets, introduced perhaps as early as the sixteenth century, became a popular feature. A number of cupboards with three sections, a sixteenth- and seventeenth-century style, were made with tambour sliding doors. Later, in the nineteenth century, these three-section cupboards reverted to having fixed plain-wood panel open-and-shut doors, with decoration limited to high polishing and insertion of metal lockplates, hinges and occasional medallion plaques. In both centuries there also appeared the wooden 'room-dividing' type of stand, though the dimensions of some of these were hardly large enough for that role. The stand below is clearly for displaying ornaments.

Like the Chinese, the Japanese continued throughout the eighteenth century and for the first three quarters of the nineteenth to make traditional pieces, maintaining what Western specialists are swift to admit were consistently high standards of craftsmanship and lacquering skill. They continued to use the short cabriole leg

17th cent. Japanese display stand and cupboard, sometimes used as a room divider.

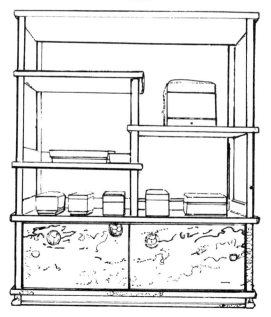

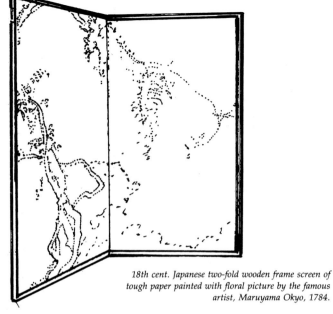

18th cent. Japanese two-fold wooden frame screen of tough paper painted with floral picture by the famous artist, Maruyama Okyo, 1784.

on low tables, and on stands for cabinets. Perhaps the main developments occurred in screens, of which the Japanese produced an enormous quantity and variety at this period, many of them painted by the most accomplished Japanese artists. The robust paper on which the pictorial work was done lasted for a long time. There is a fine two-fold panel screen of about 1784 in Bristol's City Art Gallery, by Maruyama Okyo.

Japanese craftsmen meanwhile continued to make fine furniture, with exquisite lacquer decoration. For a long time in previous centuries, particularly in the feudal period under the shoguns, topics in the decoration had had a military slant, with portrayals of weaponry and protective foliage, but in the eighteenth and nineteenth centuries many of the motifs became more peaceful, with birds, paeonies and rustic scenes.

Another interesting feature of Japanese furniture craft, which did not originate in the period but which seems to have become fashionable in the eighteenth and nineteenth centuries was the production of various kinds of stand for clothes, utensils and so forth. The kimono rack, probably devised a millennium earlier, received interesting treatment of lacquer and metal mounts. Other types of stand could be assembled from parts when needed and dismantled and stacked away when not in use.

Above, 18th cent. Indo-Chinese (possibly Cambodian) lacquered cabinet with drawers and with centre cupboards of two doors each.

Right, 18th cent. Siamese library cupboard decorated with black lacquer and gilt ornament. Height, 51½ ins. Note slightly trapezoid shape.

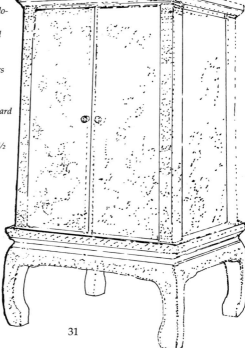

In other parts of South East Asia, such as Thailand, Cambodia and Vietnam, furniture tended to emulate styles from China, and less often from Japan. But there were other influences, too. An eighteenth-century library cupboard from Thailand, now in the National Museum in Copenhagen, has Chinese-style inward-turning feet on its stand, the shape of the cupboard itself is slightly trapezoid, narrower at the top, which is probably a local variant, and it has gilt ornament that is in places suggestive of Islamic design. In Burma, furniture began to be decorated with lacquer as far back as the thirteenth century, and some fine eighteenth-century pieces have survived, demonstrating the long tradition of high skill in that process.

EUROPE

(1) ANCIENT GREECE AND ROME

Ancient Greek furniture appears to have been the earliest to develop more than one distinct style. The first style, from about the tenth to the sixth centuries BC, was an upright, rigid and rectilinear one, much like Assyrian and ancient Persian styles (see page 13). Animal hooves for feet, straight armrests and stiff, perpendicular backs, characterized chairs. Beds and couches stood high off the ground, though there are the beginnings of more luxurious upholstery and cushioning. These centuries were times of oligarchic rule in Greece, and there may be a link between this and Greek furniture of the period.

In the fifth century, the Greeks, already locked in a struggle to the death with the Persians who coveted the wealth of Greek cities, began to experiment with different and more democratic forms of government, in the hope that this would stimulate the national desire to remain independent. This was accompanied by a great liberation of artistic spirit and energy, which sought expression away from the influence of the Near East, and it was reflected visually in new architecture, sculpture and ceramics, and also in furniture which began to break away from the past. We see the emergence of free flowing curves producing a more relaxed appearance and function in pieces like chairs, couches and tables, and an expanding reliance on upholstery and drapes. Couches, for example, were closer to the floor, tables, now square, rectangular and circular, had more interesting legs and feet, particularly the small round tables on tripods of animal-motif legs. Stools became taller, for sitting on instead of resting the feet, and these were of fixed and folding kinds. Armchairs and upright chairs also reflected interesting changes. One new style which was to be taken up again with great enthusiasm long afterwards in the eighteenth century was what is sometimes known as the *klismos*.

The *klismos* was sabre-legged, front and back. The idea was not entirely original. Hittite stone reliefs show similarities with Greek thrones, having sabre legs. The back members of the Greek version were gracefully curved and extended upwards to support a curved cresting rail. The seat rails were mortised into the legs, giving the legs a measure of elasticity that allowed the chair to remain steady on rough ground and which prevented it being tipped over backwards or forwards.

5th cent. BC Greek marble gravestone showing a fine example of a klismos.

33

The chair back height varied: the lower set variety let the sitter turn and use the back as an armrest; the higher kind was for more formal sitting.

We are fortunate in having a variety of remains of Roman furniture items, many of which have been found in the Italian peninsula. Some are the bronze parts of furniture that was made from part bronze, part wood, as in a variety of couches and tables, which has enabled accurate reconstructions to be made. Some remains were discovered in the ruins of Pompeii and Herculaneum, two neighbouring towns in southern Italy that were destroyed in the great eruption of the volcano Vesuvius in AD 79, whose lava covered extensive areas and thus preserved them. These were first excavated in the 18th century after discovery in 1748, and work has been going on there ever since. Other surviving Roman furniture such as tripod tables, armchairs and couches, were made of stone or marble, and many such pieces were modelled on earlier or contemporary wood and metal originals. These stone versions would have been used in gardens, perhaps even in some houses. The items, whether in wood, metal or stone, were frequently direct copies of earlier Greek forms.

1st cent. AD Roman tripod table (restored), found at Pompeii.

Roman furniture makers used a variety of woods, among which were citrus, cedar, olivewood and oak. They were expert at veneering and inlay work, and appear to have dyed certain woods to get variations in colour. They also inlaid pieces with ivory, silver, gold and tortoiseshell. Roman wood craftsmen were often fine carvers, and their metal and stone sculptors produced work of the highest artistry. Table legs, chair backs and arms, cupboard friezes and cornices, and so forth were often very fine.

One of the main pieces of Roman furniture was the bed or couch (*lectus*). This was for sleeping on at night, reclining on at dinner, sitting at to read and write, and even for receiving visitors. Most Roman beds were singles (*lectuli*), but there were double beds (*lecti geniales*), and there are Latin text references to beds for six people

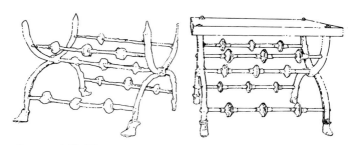

Roman period in N.W. Europe (1st–5th cent. AD) cross-legged iron table, or stool. The bosses were of brass and the feet had bronze sandals. Above is a reconstruction.

at a time! Some beds were made of bronze or more usually of wood (mostly oak, maple or arbor vitae). Some wooden frames had bronze legs and feet, some metal frames had ivory feet. The upholstery consisted of strips of webbing interwoven across the frame to support a mattress, and a bolster stuffed with wool or with swan's or duck's down.

The other main furniture items were tables, chairs, benches and stools. Tables (*mensae*), usually small and low-level, stood on three or four adjustable or folding legs, and had circular tops of wood, bronze or marble (the poet Horace wrote of owning a table of white marble). Semi-circular tables (*mensae lunatae*) for standing against a wall, were used to support a number of wooden shelves for displaying family trophies. There were chairs of various kinds: the *thronus* was an armchair with a heavily decorated back; the *cathedra* had a sloping back; and there was the barrel type, sometimes made of wicker-work. There were benches and stools (*subselliae*), one notable type being the magistrate's portable folding X-shaped type, the *sella curulis*, which was made of wood, or ivory, or as a special honour for Julius Caesar, said to have been of gold, but which was more probably of wood or ivory sheathed in gold leaf.

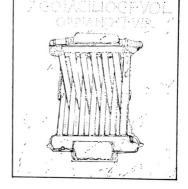

2nd or 3rd cent. AD stone commemorating a Roman imperial magistrate depicts his sella curulis, *a folding stool.*

(2) MEDIAEVAL: BYZANTINE AND GOTHIC (to c.AD1500)

For centuries after the collapse of the Western Roman Empire in the late fifth century AD, there is no clear picture of the development of individual domestic furniture styles in Western Europe. Constantinople was the capital of the Eastern Roman Empire and also of the Christian Church, and such very few pieces of furniture as may be dated and attributed to Western Europe were influenced by Byzantine furniture styles. In some cases they may have been made by Byzantine craftsmen. Among these are a sixth century bishop's throne of ivory at Ravenna in Italy, and a bronze throne supposedly made in about 600 and used by the Frankish king, Dagobert I (628–39).

In the Eastern Roman Empire, meanwhile, the craft of furniture-making continued, with the emphasis becoming more ecclesiastical, and at the same time reflecting the older traditions of the Near East. The graceful and relaxed contours of classical Greece and Rome furniture gave way to a return to upright, rigid and uncomfortable lines, such as the Ravenna throne, which itself was closer to ancient Persian thrones. But if the gracefulness diminished, the carving and the embellishment retained their high quality, in some instances standing comparison with the best Roman work. And when the process of silk manufacture, for centuries a Chinese secret that no Westerner had hitherto been able to discover, was finally revealed in the mid-sixth century by two Byzantine monks who had smuggled some silk-worm eggs out of China and brought them to Constantinople, silk-weaving leapt into importance as an industry. Silk became perhaps the most sought-after material for the drapery and upholstery of furniture.

Left, late 6th cent. Byzantine ivory throne, now at Ravenna, Italy.

Below, 6th cent. mosaic picture of a Byzantine table.

When furniture making as a skill re-emerged in Western Europe, the earliest pieces of any merit were ecclesiastical, and for the most part were fixed items, such as stalls, prayer benches, etc. in early churches. Gradually, more attention was paid to moveable articles like stools, chests and caskets.

Possibly the most widely used stools were of the folding kind, that derived from the old Roman *sella curulis* (magistrate's stool, see page 35). By now, folding stools were employed for ceremonial, ecclesiastical, military and even educational use. The bronze Dagobert throne (whose back was added several centuries later) was of X-shape, folding on the centre pivot where the X was formed. These folding stools or chairs were often made of expensive woods, or of metals, and were highly decorated. Several mediaeval manuscript illustrations show kings or dukes sitting on versions of the folding stool, while there is still in existence a chair supported on an X-shape frame, of the 16th century, on which Mary I (Queen of England, 1553–58) is believed to have sat at her wedding with Philip of Spain in Winchester Cathedral in 1554.

When a feudal system of land ownership began to evolve in Western Europe in the seventh and eighth centuries, lords began to accumulate valuable domestic possessions, such as rich clothing, jewellery, eating utensils and drinking vessels of gold, silver and copper. Some had collected relics which were of special spiritual or sentimental value. The nature of their way of life – lords had to travel incessantly about their often extensive territories – involved frequent cartage of these treasures, and that led to a demand for boxes or caskets for carrying them. Caskets could be of any size from a small box four or five inches cubed to a large one just manageable by one man. The peripatetic existence of feudal lords also generated the need for stronger boxes, which we call chests. These usually had to accommodate easily dismantled seats or beds, wall hangings, cushions, rugs and other paraphernalia that accompanied lords on the move.

For centuries, an enormous variety of casket and chest of many shapes and sizes was produced in every corner of Europe, and

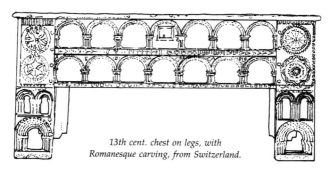

13th cent. chest on legs, with
Romanesque carving, from Switzerland.

there have been some fascinating survivors. Many were embellished with very fine carving or other ornament. Some were banded with decorative iron strapwork, and the earliest even had iron locks and clasps. Lids were flat, domed or gabled; if flat, the chests could be used as seats when not being transported. Eventually, some chests were made to stand on legs which were extensions of the vertical end members (stiles); this was the beginning of the form which chests took all over Europe from the thirteenth and fourteenth centuries right into the nineteenth century.

One piece of furniture that came into general use in ecclesiastical, royal and baronial circles was the cupboard, in two forms, one with shelves and one with hanging space. The earliest cupboards were often crudely put together, and many were painted with portraits or figures in vivid colours, which hide the indifferent workmanship at the joints. These were on the whole not easily moved about, like chests and stools, and there is little evidence of cupboards being made so that they could be readily dismantled.

Well-known 13th cent. Austrian sacristy cupboard, decorated with paint on plaster, at Halberstadt Cathedral.

Indeed, it is clear that many cupboards were inset into walls in much the same way that seats and benches were built as part of the wood panelling of a room in an important building.

The Gothic style of architecture emerged in north-western Europe as early as the mid-to-late eleventh century: among the earliest examples were L'Abbaye-Aux-Hommes at Caen, in France, and Durham Cathedral, in England. But it is probably right to say that Gothic did not fasten its grip upon European architecture and building in general until the end of the twelfth century. The new style, with its many fascinating regional variations, influenced, again regionally as well as continentally, the design of both church and domestic furniture, at first in cathedrals and important churches, great castles and palaces, and later on in smaller churches, houses and cottages. Sadly, there is very little extant furniture outside churches in Gothic style that can safely be dated to before about 1300, and illuminations in mediaeval manuscripts do not help to fill the gap.

Probably the commonest piece of furniture from this period is the chest and its variants, of which there are a few late thirteenth-century examples, a few more fourteenth-century specimens, and many from the fifteenth century. Chests were usually decorated on the flat surfaces, particularly on the front, with ecclesiastical motifs, such as tracery, pointed arching, foliage, finials, figures of knights and so forth, a custom continued in some areas right into the mid-sixteenth century. The French chest illustrated below dates from the end of the thirteenth century and is typically Gothic in decoration. A popular additional motif on the chest front was a coat of arms, or just a shield, and this sometimes indicated for whom the chest was originally made.

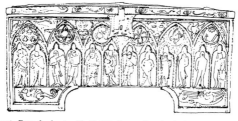

13th cent. French chest with Gothic decoration, including a row of knightly figures.

The quality of construction of some of these early chests shows great skill on the part of mediaeval carpenters. Though some were of what we call boarded construction, that is, assemblages of planks nailed at the ends, joinery had emerged as a woodcraft skill before the fourteenth century and had begun to be employed by craftsmen making box furniture and seat furniture for rich patrons, religious and secular. In quite early times, pieces assumed architectural proportions, and were embellished with architectural ornament.

Some chests were lidded boxes that lay flat on the ground or were put on trestles or alcove shelves. Othere were constructed with legs or feet as part of the framework (usually extensions of the vertical corner members) to raise them above damp floors. Many of the oldest surviving chests, such as the late thirteenth-century example at the Musée Carnavalet in Paris, the fourteenth-century chest at the Kunstgewerbemuseum in Berlin and the late thirteenth-century Swedish chest from Voxthorp have legs or feet. Others were fitted with feet or sledges at later dates.

We have seen that simple cupboards were already being made in the earlier mediaeval period. In Gothic times, these became more elaborately decorated. There also emerged, as extensions of

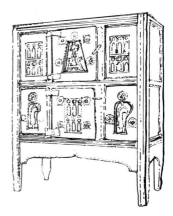

Left, 15th cent. French oak dressoir with tracery and linenfold decoration. The centre cupboard part can be locked, to protect valuable utensils.
Below, late 15th cent. English oak livery cupboard.

the cupboard, furniture expressly designed to store and to display valuable items like good pottery and plate. This appeared in various forms, such as the stand of graded open shelves and the stand which also incorporated a closed compartment or two (the *dressoir*, or *dressouer*), both types developing in some examples into the most splendid pieces. In England, the stand (the number of whose shelves is said to have related to the owner's status) came to be called the cup-board (as distinct from cupboard), which meant a piece of furniture for storing and displaying quality vessels and utensils. Some of the best display furniture of the late Middle Ages was produced in the rich towns of the Low Countries.

The Gothic period also saw the development of seat furniture. Most people sat on stools, settles or benches, or on cushions on the floor or on chests. The chair was on the whole a rarity, reserved for the master of a house, a tradition that persisted into the sixteenth century. It is from this that we get the word 'chairman' for the head of an organization. Usually, the chair was an armchair, sometimes placed on a dais to elevate the sitter above the rest of the room's company. Armchairs were of two main kinds: the throne type, which already existed in the early Middle Ages, with decorated panelled back and sometimes sides as well, and the backstool adaptation. A famous example of a Gothic armchair of the throne variety is the Coronation Chair in Westminster Abbey, made in c.1300.

The other important piece of furniture produced in a variety of interesting styles was the bed. In north-western Europe, prosperous householders owned one or more beds, over each of which was raised a canopy, or tester (from the French *tête*, meaning head) draped with curtains. At the head was a headboard, often of solid panelling with fine carving, sometimes in linenfold motif. In warmer countries, the draperies were not needed, and beds often had no more than an attractively painted headboard and footboard.

By the end of the mediaeval period, different parts of Europe were enjoying individual vogues of furniture design, using alternative woods. In France, walnut became widely fashionable, while oak persisted in England and Germany. In Scandinavia, pine and birch were more readily available.

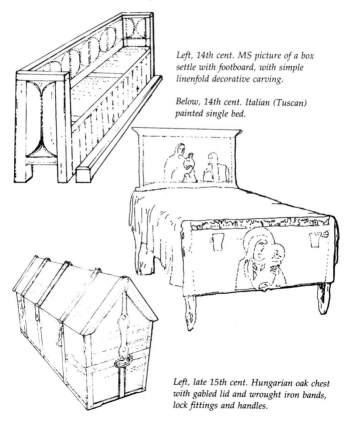

Left, 14th cent. MS picture of a box settle with footboard, with simple linenfold decorative carving.

Below, 14th cent. Italian (Tuscan) painted single bed.

Left, late 15th cent. Hungarian oak chest with gabled lid and wrought iron bands, lock fittings and handles.

(3) ITALY: FIFTEENTH TO NINETEENTH CENTURIES

The Renaissance originated in Italy in the fourteenth century. Loosely put, it was a revival in Europe of Greek and Roman ideals in art, literature, architecture and sculpture, and it was to spread, with varying intensity, throughout the countries of Europe. This return to classical ideas affected the design of furniture, but the limited evidence about what sort of furniture Greeks and Romans used restricted Renaissance craftsmen in its reconstruction. There were very few relics of classical furniture, and they were woefully incomplete. What was known was to be found more from surviving descriptions in literature or portrayal in sculpture and stone relief, painted ceramics and so forth. These were not very helpful. Furniture makers tried to improve on these morsels of information by making them conform to their interpretation of the principles and proportions of classical architecture, particularly with larger pieces, but they did not add significantly to the variety of articles that could be regarded as furniture. While in the great palaces that were springing up in or near the main cities such as Rome, Florence, Venice, Genoa and Milan, the decorations of the huge rooms inside were rich and spectacular, with marble floors, gilded ceilings, and flooded with opulent fabrics, the range of furniture was small, with only beds, chairs, tables, chests, sideboards and cupboards figuring in typical inventories of the time, and often, not many of any of these six items being in the lists. The house-owners' wealth and taste were far more sharply displayed in the objects that they possessed, on open surfaces or in cupboards and drawers, such as gold and silver plate, jewellery, coins, paintings, statues and books.

Much of the furniture produced was seldom as dramatic as the architecture on which it was sometimes modelled, though there are very fine exceptions. The di Giovanni cupboard, made in about 1500 and now at the Abbazia di Monte Oliveto Maggiore, near Siena, not only epitomizes the best in Italian Renaissance furniture design according to architectural principles. It is also a very good example of *intarsia* work. This technique, which originated in mediaeval Italy, became highly developed in the late fifteenth century, particularly in Florence, where one of its greatest exponents was Francesco di Giovanni. *Intarsia* is a form of wood marquetry which is made up from polygonal blocks of wood, bone, mother-of-pearl, stone or metal arranged in geometric patterns. To obtain contrasting colours and shades, the materials were sometimes dyed or scorched. A development of *intarsia* was the *trompe d'œil* form, by which the illusion of a three-dimensional picture, with an element of perspective, was created.

To take one or two furniture categories of the period, Italian craftsmen produced modifications of the folding stool, which for centuries has been limited to a seat supported by two pairs of crossed members articulating at the centre of the 'X'. It now had a row of crossed leg members close together on both sides, and the

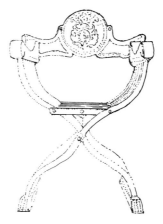

Early 16th cent. Italian Renaissance X-shaped chair

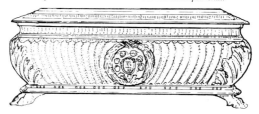

Early 16th cent. Italian Renaissance cassone *from Tuscany*

legs extended upwards above the seat in graceful curves, and were joined at or near the top by a carved back. These stools resembled the old Roman *sella curulis* (see page 35) from which they were partly derived. The chest, the coffer and the box seat were all improved. A chest now acquired architectural features such as a cornice, a plinth, and, sometimes, side pilasters, and bore elaborate carved decoration. The piece was called a *cassone*. Many *cassoni* were made from walnut which, when stained and varnished, took on a soft, dark brown hue that enhanced their outline. There were also box seats, which were similar to *cassoni*, but which had a back, and had the seat lifting as a lid to reveal storage space. In this form the piece is known as a *cassapanca*.

Tables for dining or working at had rectangular tops which were supported at each end by large, elaborate consoles, sometimes connected by a highly carved stretcher, possibly with a third console of similar design placed centrally beneath the top. Console feet took the form of animal (particularly lion) paws, or cherubic figures, or sometimes grotesques.

Towards the end of the sixteenth century, new varieties of furniture began to appear, including the bureau-cabinet with fall front, and the first round-top tables on four or six legs. Chairs, normally on straight, square section legs, received decorative carving on arms, backs and stretchers, and often on seat rails as well. Velvet cushions, or velvet- or leather-covered stuffed seats made chairs more comfortable. But there was no move towards resurrecting the design of the relaxing Greek sabre-leg chair (*klismos*).

Italian Renaissance furniture forms began to attract attention all over Europe, where they were absorbed into national furniture-making traditions. In the North-West, they gradually superseded the prevailing Gothic forms. The focus on architecture, which led to greater attention being paid to interior decoration and furnishing as an integrated concept, prepared the ground for many national styles of furniture on the Continent.

In the seventeenth century, Italy was to become the source of the Baroque style of architecture and the furniture that followed. Even before the turn of the century, the restraint of the classical lines in Renaissance furniture was becoming submerged beneath exuberant ornament, with mass foliage, curving contours, heavy scrollings, plastic forms and so forth. Tables and some types of cabinet, for example, began to be supported on painted or gilded sub-structures with carved naked figures of naiads, negroes,

Mid-17th cent. Italian style cabinet-on-stand, with Florentine pietre dure *panels by Domenico Benotti, bought by the English diarist John Evelyn who had the cabinet made to accommodate them.*

44

eagles, lions and dolphins, jumbled up with shells, cartouches and swags. Table tops consisted of brilliantly coloured marble slab, marble mosaic or *pietre dure* work. This last is a decorative treatment composed of hard, semi-precious stones of different colours cut and fitted in patterns and polished smooth. It was not a new technique, but it played an important role in the seventeenth century upsurge of spending on decoration and furnishing by a growing number of wealthy grand home owners who commissioned every kind of luxurious ornamentation. *Pietre dure* was also used in decorating cabinet fronts.

Chairs were elaborately carved and gilded, with exaggerated figures or motifs, especially on arms and legs, and in some cases actually serving as legs. They were upholstered in a range of new, costly velvets, silks and other fabrics. Wardrobes became massive and architectural, console tables were supported on prolifically sculptured bases, and for the first time cabinet-makers produced bookcases in splendid forms with columns, statues and figures along the cornice and elsewhere. Many great homes had elaborate globes, of the Earth as it was then understood, and of the stars in the firmament. Another decorative treatment, known in the sixteenth century but very much more popular in the later seventeenth, was *scagliola* work, an imitation of marble made from pulverized marble bonded with an agent to give a veined effect. It could take a high polish. *Scagliola* was also made to resemble *pietre dure*, but was much less expensive to produce.

Some of the best examples of Baroque furniture were inspired by the painter and designer Pietro da Cortona (1596–1669), who supervised the decoration of the Pitti Palace in Florence and the Barberini Palace in Rome, in the mid-seventeenth century. Much Baroque furniture was made in walnut, marked by fine veneered surfaces with contrasting raised panelling and moulding. Cupboard pediments were embellished with gay carved ornament along top and sides. In Venice, a leading centre of furniture-making, contrasts were often achieved by part-gilding the wood. Venice was also a centre for lacquered furniture. Lacquering had first become a popular decorative treatment in Rome in the early part of the century; by the 1660s Venetian craftsmen were producing fine black and vermilion lacquerwork, with raised gold chinoiserie subjects, and towards the end of the century they were using new colours, such as dark green.

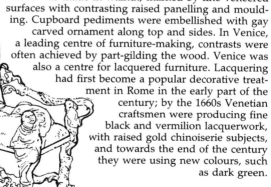

Late 17th cent. Italian upholstered armchair by the Venetian sculptor and designer, Andrea Brustolon (c.1690s).

One of the most influential figures during the last two decades of the century was Andrea Brustolon (1662–1732), the Venetian wood sculptor and decorator. Creator of many famous religious carvings, he also produced elaborately decorated chairs, looking-glass frames (in which he specialized), vase stands and candle stands. His work bridges the seventeenth and eighteenth centuries, and by the time of his death he had already become attracted to the French Rococo styles at a time when other Italian craftsmen were still clinging to the Baroque.

At the beginning of the eighteenth century, Italy was still divided into kingdoms and states whose quarrels and shifts in alliances with bigger European powers were affecting trade and, to some extent, material wealth. Many top Italian craftsmen emigrated to work in France, Britain and Germany. Furniture in Italy, meanwhile, was still stylistically regionalized, and it is quite possible to see differences between the treatments of pieces from, say, Venice and Rome, or Turin and Florence. The main furniture-making centres were still largely in the northern half of the country where many leading designers spent some if not all their careers, as at Turin [the architect Filippo Juvarra (1676–1736) and Pietro Piffetti (1700–77), probably the first real Italian *ébéniste*] for example, at Genoa [Antonio-Maria Maragliano (1664–1739), and Domenico Parodi (1668–1740)], and at Venice [Andrea Brustolon (1662–1732), and Antonio Corradini (1668–1752)]. Venice continued to produce perhaps the best, and certainly the most exciting furniture.

Drawing for an Italian console table by Filippo Juvarra of Turin, c.1730.

The Venetian craftsmen were among the earliest to adopt the French Rococo styles, at the end of the 1720s. They also specialized in gilding walnut furniture and adorning surfaces with pieces of coloured glass. In the first half of the century, lacquerwork continued to be produced on an extensive scale. Chinese patterns began to give way to native Italian landscapes and figures, often done in lighter colours like pale blue and pale green, but also in another style in much darker green, with prominent gold decoration. This love of lacquer spilled over into imitations, polychrome painting of furniture all over in brilliant colours, and a cheap version called *lacca contrafatta*, was introduced. This was achieved by applying paper cut-outs of scenes to woodwork, painting them brightly and then varnishing the piece all over. Most of this type of work was done for more 'down-market' customers.

One growingly fashionable piece of furniture was the *commode*, in which Italian craftsmen carried the *bombé* effect (see page 147) to such extremes that no French *ébéniste* would have considered them acceptable, and Rococo *commodes*, as well as other pieces, continued to be made right up to the 1780s. When the Rococo was finally played out in Italy in the 1780s, its place was taken by what we might call Italian Louis XVI. Even here, however, there were regional differences. In the north, the influence of the Louis XVI style was an Italian interpretation of the neo-classical straight from France. Further south, the restrained neo-classical style already popular in Britain as a result of the work of Robert Adam and others (see page 105), came to bear on many pieces. In both northern and southern Italy, this move towards the neo-classical style was encouraged by the paintings and engravings of celebrated artists, notably Giovanni Battista Piranesi (1720–78), and by the pattern books of Giovanni Albertolli (the only pattern books of furniture designs available in Italy in the eighteenth century). Among prominent craftsmen working in the Louis XVI style were Giuseppe Maggiolini (1738–1814) of Milan and Giuseppe Maria Bonzanigo (1744–1820) of Turin, who produced remarkable cabinets, bureaux and *commodes*.

Mid-17th cent. Italian Rococo style green and gold lacquered two-drawer commode, *from Venice.*

Late 18th cent. Italian neo-Classical style inlaid three-drawer commode *by Giuseppe Maggiolini of Milan, and signed by him.*

Early 19th cent. Italian Empire style mahogany writing table by Giovanni Socchi (1807), with gilt bronze mounts. Though unattractive, it is ingenious, as it opens out to form a table with paper-rack and a desk chair.

By the early nineteenth century, much Italian furniture had become less formal than strict Louis XVI style, and pieces were being made with elaborate decoration in paintwork, gilding and marquetry. Furniture-makers in northern Italy continued to take their cue from France, adopting the Directoire style and its successor, the Empire style (see page 64). These, combined with a slight harking back to classical details stimulated by excavations at Pompeii and Herculaneum which had begun around 1748, resulted in interesting Italian Empire furniture, with carving and decoration of great technical skill. Walnut was still employed on a wide scale, but there was far less gilt-bronze ornament. Some of the pieces could be regarded as unattractive, such as the well-known writing desk made for Napoleon's sister by Giovanni Socchi of Florence. But the style remained a major feature of Italian furniture, especially in the north, for much of the century. One or two quite extraordinary chairs, for example, were made in the 1840s, with arms in the shape of crouched swans, and birds' wings elsewhere in the supports. Round tables were set on elaborate lyre-type pedestals, and, as in examples now in the Pitti Palace in Florence, winged figures supported gilt-bronze decorated tables. As the movement towards Italian unity (the *Risorgimento*) gathered momentum in the 1840s and 1850s, there was a return to some Renaissance styles in furniture. In some quarters it was labelled Dantesque, and it boasted new versions of the classically inspired X-shaped chair, now upholstered in luxurious red, heavy carved tables, and a spate of profusely carved *cassoni*.

(4) FRANCE: SIXTEENTH TO NINETEENTH CENTURIES

Renaissance to Baroque

Although France had been the home of the Gothic style since the eleventh century, it was not slow to accept the new ideas of the Renaissance, certainly among royalty, nobility and rich merchants.

This enthusiasm was greatly encouraged by the ostentatious and sometimes vainglorious French military expeditions against Italy led by three kings of France in succession, Charles VIII (1483–98), Louis XII (1498–1515) and François I (1515–47), which brought France directly if violently into contact with Renaissance splendours. François I, a man of considerable taste in the arts, encouraged Italian architects, artists and craftsmen to come to France and work in Paris, in the Loire Valley and at Fontainebleau, some 38 miles south of Paris, where he planned to enlarge and beautify the royal residence there. Two leading men he employed at Fontainebleau were Giovanni Batista Rosso and Francesco Primaticcio, who were painters and sculptors as well as designers, and through them, as much as anyone else François I attracted from Italy, Renaissance ideas impressed themselves on French art and architecture, merging with the Gothic style rather than displacing it.

At this time, craftsmen working in Paris and at the châteaux of the Loire began to use indigenous walnut in place of oak. Its colour when polished was like shining bronze, while its fine grain made it easier to carve. We see also the introduction of Italian *intarsia* (see page 42) and its development into the beginnings of wood marquetry of which French craftsmen were to become the supreme exponents in the eighteenth century.

In the middle of the sixteenth century the works of Vitruvius, the ancient Roman architect, appeared in print at Strasbourg. They

Late 16th cent. French tester bed based on a design by du Cerceau.

were the earliest copies available outside Italy and their appearance coincided with the emergence of the first pattern books for furniture and decoration in France. One, by Corrozet, described and illustrated a variety of pieces of furniture in great French houses, made in the first half of the century. Jacques Androuet du Cerceau (1515–84), who worked for François I at Fontainebleau, produced a number of illustrated books on architecture and furniture, as did Hughes Sambin (c.1520–c.1601) who worked at Dijon. These and others exerted a strong influence on French furniture styles over the second half of the sixteenth century and into the seventeenth. Craftsmen produced very fine carving, low reliefs, incised flowers, foliage, scroll-work and caryatids. Emphasis was laid on the making of two-tiered cupboards, cabinets, elaborate tables and canopied beds. Most of this furniture was made in walnut, but more expensively some were in ebony veneer, which required special skills and which led to the creation of a society of craftsmen called *ébénistes*, a term that in Louis XIV's time came to be applied exclusively to makers of cabinet furniture. The term *menuisiers* had already and for long meant craftsmen who made solid wood pieces like chairs and boarded furniture.

While the merging of Gothic and Renaissance styles proved successful in Paris and other main towns in central and southern France, older and starker traits of the Gothic style persisted in the north where there was a stubborn adherence to oak.

Seventeeth-century French furniture may be divided into two main periods, viz. c.1600–c.1661 and c.1661–c.1700. The earlier period was influenced both by late Italian Renaissance ideas and by contemporary Flemish styles. A distinctly national French style had not yet emerged. Part of this was due to the long and demoralizing internal wars of religion (1562–98) which stifled creative development, along with much else. After the Edict of Nantes (1598), which ended the wars, national pride had a chance to revive, under the constructive rule of Henry IV (1589–1610) who appreciated the value of encouraging the arts as well as commerce and manufacture. He invited Italian and Flemish craftsmen to Paris and gave them workshops in the Louvre* and elsewhere. French craftsmen meanwhile were persuaded to go abroad to learn foreign techniques, particularly in Italy and Flanders. This was a shot in the arm for French craftsmanship, whose achievements Henri IV did not live to see. His widow, Marie dei Medici, a Florentine duchess, continued to encourage the arts, and in the 1620s invited the great Flemish painter Rubens to advise her on the decoration of her new palace of Luxembourg in Paris which de Brosse was building for her in Renaissance style. Rubens also painted twenty-five huge canvasses commemorating her activities.

---

* Among those with workshops in the Louvre were Michel Campe, Jean Macé (who introduced the art of ebony veneering to France) and Pierre Boulle, father of Andre-Charles Boulle (see page 53).

New ideas about furniture began to emerge. The Italian taste for *intarsia* and *pietre dure*, and the Flemish skill in wood marquetry and veneering, and painting on wood, were absorbed by French craftsmen, and in particular their cabinets-on-stands reflect this. Chairs, now more widely used, became more important pieces of furniture and households had more of them, and emphasis was now placed on rich upholstery. Special wool-based fabrics called moquettes, were produced. Chair seats were overstuffed and covered with embroidered cloth bordered with gold braid and brass studs. Fifteenth- and sixteenth-century styles of cup-board and dressoir evolved into a growingly practical and yet highly aesthetic variety of cabinets. There was also a demand for *armoires* (wardrobes).

Further encouragement to French architecture and craftsman-ship came from the government of Cardinal Richelieu (1585–1642), who was chief minister to Louis XIII from 1624 to 1642, and who commissioned furnishings for the court and for his own palaces in Paris, and in the country. Cabinets were decorated with tor-toiseshell and ebony, tables were topped with thick marble slabs inset with *pietre dure*, smaller tables on decorated turned legs were joined at low level by H- and X-form stretchers, and before the end of the period we see the emergence of the table with drawers on either side of a kneehole, called the *bureau*, but which was not at first used exclusively for writing.

Richelieu's successor, Cardinal Mazarin, was Italian by birth, and preferred Italian decorative styles which had already moved on from Renaissance and Mannerist styles to the Baroque, with its free use of curves within the classical framework of the orders of architecture, and which he championed in works executed for court and state. This had a considerable effect upon the development of French furniture styles, but as with French architecture, French furniture of the latter half of the seventeenth century was in the Baroque style but with more restrained lines and less ornamental exuberance.

Early 17th cent. French Louis XIII period bureau in red tortoiseshell and copper decoration, on eight legs.

This became more evident after the death of Mazarin in 1661, when Louis XIV, now 23 years old, decided to rule France himself.

Louis set out to make Paris the intellectual and artistic centre of Europe. This naturally included decoration and furnishing, and to that end he decided to reorganize the Crown Furniture to give the lead. He appointed Jean Baptiste Colbert (1619–1683), one of Mazarin's ablest assistants, as controller-general of finances, with a brief, among other things, to ensure that there was enough money to attract to Paris the best available artists and craftsmen. He also made Colbert Superintendent of the King's Buildings. They set up a state organization called *La Manufacture royale des meubles de la Couronne*, with premises at the Gobelins factory area on the outskirts of Paris, where there were already a number of craft workshops. At its head they put Charles Le Brun (1619–90), one of the leading artists of the day. He was appointed chief painter to the king and was commissioned to supervise the decoration and furnishing of the new palace that the king proposed to build around his father's old hunting lodge at Versailles, along with other buildings already in use or on the drawing board. The decorations, furnishings, tapestries and paintings for Versailles were to be produced in the Gobelins. 'These workshops acted like crucibles, producing the designs which paved the way for a new period of French furniture.'* One of the earliest cabinet-makers (*ébénistes*) to be attracted from abroad was the Italian Domenico Cucci (*c*.1635–1705), who arrived sometime before the Gobelins reorganization. He soon became the leading wood sculptor and *ébéniste*, and was to do much to make the highly decorated cabinet the most fashionable piece of furniture of the time. Two of his pieces are the pair of *grands cabinets* now at Alnwick Castle, in Northumberland: they were delivered to Louis XIV in 1683 and cost him 16,000 livres. Cucci produced the most remarkable decorative treatments, using inlays of pewter, lapis lazuli, gilded tortoiseshell, bronze, encrusted stone, mosaics and so forth.

Le Brun personally controlled the work of the *Manufacture* and provided most of the designs for it, and it has been said that for a generation little emerged that did not carry the mark of his genius. The Gobelins won the highest renown and the craftsmen who worked there earned more than those of any other furniture-making centre in Europe. On his death in 1690, Le Brun was succeeded by Jean Bérain (1638–1711), a great artist and designer who did more than any to advance the taste for the Rococo style. By that time, *ébénistes, menuisiers* and bronze-workers had started to work independently of the state, producing furniture to their own designs. Two bronze-workers' guilds operated at the time: the *fondeurs-ciseleurs* who cast and roughly chased the bronzes, and the

* Pierre Verlet, *French Royal Furniture*. English translation, Barrie & Rockliffe, 1963.

ciseleurs-doreurs who finely chased and gilded them. Not all bronzes were gilded.

Apart from cabinets, other fashionable pieces were chests, consoles, day-beds, armchairs (*fauteuils*) and tables. The last-named were made for a great variety of uses – one of Louis XIV's inventories of royal furniture includes folding tables, flat-topped tables with a filing cabinet on top, card-tables, dressing tables, and even tables for taking meals in the bedroom. One new piece was a type of *bureau*, with fewer drawers than the seventeenth century type mentioned above (page 51), but which extend across the whole width. This was the *commode*, which was topped either with a shaped piece of marble or by cabinet work, that is, marquetry-decorated veneering. It came into use in the last quarter of the century but was not called a *commode* until 1700.

In 1672, Andre-Charles Boulle (1642–1732) was appointed cabinet-maker to the king (*ébéniste du roi*) in succession to Jean Macé. He was thirty, and was given quarters and workshops in the Louvre. Here, he developed though did not invent special decorative techniques now associated with his name, Boulle marquetry, employing tortoiseshell, pewter and brass, which remained fashionable for cabinets, *armoires*, *bureaux* and other pieces that were mainly rectilinear until the beginning of the eighteenth century, and which was copied abroad. At the Louvre, Boulle trained four of his sons as assistants, some of them eventually taking over his business. Boulle lived to be 90, long enough to see his particular style of craftsmanship go right out of fashion.

French furniture reached the peak of achievement in the eighteenth century. Styles were rich, varied and exciting, and craftsmanship was unquestionably the finest in the history of furniture. The styles fall into four clear phases: *Régence* (*c.*1710–*c.*1730); Louis XV (*c.*1730–*c.*1760); Transitional (*c.*1760–*c.*1770); and Louis XVI (*c.*1770–*c.*1795).

Late 17th cent. French Louis armoire by A-C Boulle in the brass and tortoiseshell inlay decoration associated with his name. 2.7m tall.

Régence

Historically, the *Régence* lasted from 1715–1723, but the new style had begun some years before 1715 and carried on into the fourth decade. *Régence* furniture was lighter and gayer than its predecessor: tortoiseshell and brass marquetry gave way to wood marquetry, and the asymmetrical Rococo style displaced the cornices, curves and panelling of the Baroque. Jean Bérain (1638–1711) dominated the designs for a long time. Characteristics of his style include fantastic gilt-bronze (*ormolu*) mount designs, based on shell and rock forms, with curves, scrolls and elaborate flowers and foliage, which spilled across the woodwork, generally smothering it and concealing its lines. The supreme practitioners of this style were Antoine Gaudreaux (*c*.1680–*c*.1751) and Charles Cressent (1685–1768). There were of course many others who were scarcely less accomplished.

By the eighteenth century, the *ébénistes* had already become an independent body of craftsmen, even though they were employed by the Crown and many like Boulle and Cressent made very good livings. Although their work was highly individual, it nonetheless paid homage to certain fundamental principles. They provided furniture for an immensely rich aristocracy which had more leisure than was good for it. So, the furniture made was both practical and comfortable. Legs of chairs, for example, became shorter, which gave the chairs more stability, chair backs were lower which enabled the sitter to relax, chair arms were placed further back on the seat and not directly over the front legs, which allowed the sitter to sprawl. It is unlikely that these modifications were made to accommodate either changes in women's fashions or the height of men's wigs.

The Regent, Philippe, duc d'Orléans, nephew of Louis XIV, occupied the Palais Royal in Paris and also maintained a country mansion at Bagnolet. An architect at each residence superintended

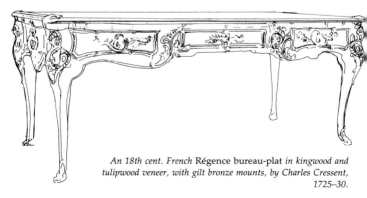

An 18th cent. French Régence bureau-plat *in kingwood and tulipwood veneer, with gilt bronze mounts, by Charles Cressent, 1725–30.*

the operations of improving the decoration and furnishing; in Paris, it was Gilles-Marie Oppenord (1672–1742), and at Bagnolet a man of very different taste, Christophe Huet (1690–1759), who was a disciple of Bérain. The principal furniture maker at both residences was for a time Charles Cressent and he in turn was inspired by various artists, chief among them Antoine Watteau (1684–1721).

Though Cressent was only one of at least fifty master craftsmen working in Paris at the time, he is a good representative, since we have catalogues of his works and accounts of his dealings with the Crown. Since each piece made by him personally would have taken months to make, there cannot have been many in his total personal repertoire during the *Régence* period, though of course he will have designed many others, and supervised assistants working on many more. Cressent rarely stamped his furniture with his name, as this had not yet become compulsory (see Appendix 2), or indeed customary. Those pieces we know are his own work are particularly fine, notably for the extensive use of Rococo gilt-bronze mounts which provided models for other *ébénistes* to follow.

During the *Régence* years, France recovered from severe economic depression following the War of the Spanish Succession (1701–13). Trade revived in many parts of the world where France had interests, particularly in the West Indies (where several islands were French possessions) and one result was the importing of exotic new woods such as mahogany, satinwood and rosewood (or kingwood). These and other woods formed basic components of marquetry which became popular after the taste for Boulle tortoiseshell and brass had declined. Gilt-bronze work continued to feature prominently on many pieces, principally protecting corners and edges, but some just for decoration. Although the two guilds, the *fondeurs-ciseleurs* and the *ciseleurs-doreurs*, had tried to monopolize gilt-bronze work, some *ébénistes* actually made their own mounts. In the next (Louis XV) period, the guilds became strong enough to stop this intrusion on their area of work, and among other *ébénistes*, Cressent was prosecuted by the guilds several times for making his own mounts.

One of the changes made to the interiors of larger houses in the eighteenth century was the provision of more and more small rooms, set aside for various activities such as sewing, writing and dressing. This created a demand for more small pieces of furniture. One was the *encoignure*, or corner-cupboard, which had originally been designed in the early 1700s. It now became a standard piece of furniture. *Encoignures* were usually made in pairs for large rooms, but also singly for smaller apartments. Another new piece was the *bonheur-du-jour*, or ladies' writing desk.

The Rococo style was considerably enlivened by new ideas from Juste-Aurèle Meissonnier (1695–1750), designer to the king from 1726, who bridged the *Régence* and Louis XV periods. Meissonnier published an extensive range of designs for decoration and furniture in asymmetrical *rocaille* form. The shell in a variety of modes became a central feature in marquetry work on carcase furniture and on solid furniture (*menuiserie*) such as chairs and settees. Chair backs now had the wooden surround of the frame prominently exposed, often featuring a central shell motif. Chairs were painted, gilded and even silvered. Many that are datable to the period but which are now in plain wood were once thus decorated.

Something should be said about the continuing vogue for lacquered furniture. As in other European countries, lacquered cabinets and chests made in the East had been imported into France and put on homemade stands. At the beginning of the eighteenth century, some *ébénistes* tried to imitate oriental lacquer-work, but at first with indifferent results. A better effect was achieved by importing oriental lacquered panels and building them into an indigenous framework. In about 1730, Guillaume Martin and his brothers were granted permission for a fixed period to market a new transparent lac varnish, mixed with pigment, that they had invented. The varnish, known as Vernis Martin, enabled *ébénistes* to produce lacquered pieces of better quality; fitted with bronze mounts, these remained popular for many years.

Louis XV

The Louis XV period saw the Rococo style rise to its height, but also witnessed the beginning of its decline. The architectural form in furniture was swamped in over-elaborate decoration with bubbling, flowing bronze-work and fantastic designs in marquetry. Even the piece shapes themselves took on exaggerated curves and angles. Bronze decor was so ornate that it obscured things like keyholes, handles, and locks. New types of furniture were introduced, some to meet the needs and oblige the whims of women, whose influence in society was growing. The excessive use of bronze-work, moreoover, meant that overall costs rocketed, in an age when court and nobles were already spending on an unprecedented scale.

Although the taste for this type of furniture owed much to Meissonnier, the Slodtz brothers and others, Louis XV himself played no small part in its success. Deeply interested in the actual design and decor of the new furniture he wanted to instal in Versailles and other royal palaces, he sketched out original ideas on paper and give them to Meissonnier or the Slodtz brothers to draw in greater detail. Later on, he liked to have small-scale models made of pieces he proposed to commission. The best *ébénistes* made furniture to his designs as well as to those of Meissonnier and others, and in many instances Jacques Caffieri (1678–1755), leading sculptor and bronze-maker, modelled the mounts, sometimes signing them. The taste extended beyond France, and Rococo was soon taken up all over Europe, in different national interpretations according to national tastes, even in Britain where, among others, Chippendale designed a number of pieces (notably chairs) with strong Rococo motifs. Before long, foreign craftsmen again began to come to Paris to set up in business and join a thriving nucleus of *ébénistes, menuisiers* and bronze-workers already there.

Louis XV styles were even more relaxed than those of the *Régence*. Sofas, day-beds and armchairs, types of furniture increasingly demanded by an indolent aristocracy, had graceful undulating lines with exquisitely carved supports and backs, upholstered in light coloured silks or printed cottons. *Bergère* chairs, with soft upholstered sides and a loose cushion, became popular. Stools were important in large reception rooms: if the king or members of his family called, it was an honour to be allowed to sit on a stool in their presence. Among the many pieces on which *ébénistes* expended their skills were *bureaux-plats*, drop-leaf desks, upright *secretaires*, and *commodes*. The *bureau-plat*, a flat table-like desk already known in the Louis XIV and *Régence* periods, now became a staple item. Though simple, it lent itself to much adornment in bronze-work. Some had the whole periphery of the top edged with gilt-bronze moulding, or brass moulding, shaped and bevelled in the serpentine or rectilinear outlines of the desk. Leather, dyed red, blue, green, yellow or black, and bordered in gold by means of special tools, was let into the top.

The *commode* was a chest with two or three drawers, or, more rarely, two main and two subsidiary drawers. The front was straight or bow-shaped, the latter called *bombé* to denote a swelling effect when that effect was pronounced. *Commodes* were decorated with marquetry, or parquetry or lacquerwork, fitted with gilt-bronze escutcheons, drawer handles and corner mounts, and in some cases additional bronze decorations. In the case of the *bombé* type, the sides often swelled outwards, too (see colour section). The top was surmounted with a marble slab, shaped and bevelled,

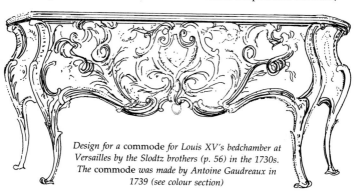

Design for a commode for Louis XV's bedchamber at Versailles by the Slodtz brothers (p. 56) in the 1730s. The commode was made by Antoine Gaudreaux in 1739 (see colour section)

the colour of the marble varying according to the colouring of the marble mantelpiece and/or other fittings in the room, for which the shape of the marble followed the outline of the *commodes*.

Earlier *commodes* had short legs fitted with gilt-bronze *sabots* (shoes) to protect the feet. Later, longer legs and shorter carcases appeared, generally with two rather than three drawers.

The *bureau-plat* was a large writing table for men. Women of Louis XV's time began to chronicle every-day events in diaries and notebooks, and some had more serious pretensions to writing. More women needed desks for themselves. The *ébénistes* obliged by designing a variety of smaller writing tables, some with mechanical devices that allowed a whole section for pens, ink and blotting sand to rise and fall at the touch of a finger. To solve the problem of having to clear things off the top of a *bureau-plat*, the *bureau à pente* appeared in about 1740. This was compact and stood on long, curving legs. It had a sloping flap which came down to horizontal for a writing surface. When closed, the desk took up little space. These desks and their companions, the *bonheurs-du-jour* and other writing tables, gave the *ébénistes* fresh opportunities for marquetry decoration. We see also the introduction of Sèvres porcelain plaques on vertical parts of the front and sides, although this kind of ornament was more popular in the period 1760–80.

Louis XV chairs were among the finest in all furniture history, combining elegance, function and comfort to an unparalleled degree, whether they were richly upholstered and ornately carved and gilded, or more simply polished and more plainly covered. Made for a variety of uses, chairs were either *fauteuils* (armchairs) or *chaises* (uprights), and had descriptive names like *fauteuil de cabinet* or *en gondole* or *à la Reine*, or *chaise d'affaires* or *à l'anglaise*.

18th cent. French Louis XV bureau à pente *in various woods made by Adrien Delorme, 1755*

18th cent. French Louis XV walnut fauteuil à la Reine *by Claude Sené, 1743*

18th cent. French Transitional encoignure in sycamore, harewood and tulipwood and with marquetry of other woods, by J-F Oeben.

Towards the end of the 1750s there was a reaction against Rococo extravagances. Straight lines re-appeared as basic features. Bronze work became less obtrusive and plainer panels of veneer competed with elaborate marquetry. Yet Rococo enthusiasts were not easily put off, and for some years there was a contest, as it were, between the two. Indeed, the Transitional period is so-named because it marked the period when the reaction gradually but definitely prevailed over Rococo.

It was in the Louis XV period that the practice of stamping furniture with makers' names became obligatory, and the procedure is summarized in Appendix 2 (page 137). It should perhaps be stated here that despite regulations, stamping was not always confined to actual makers: we know that dealers selling new pieces also stamped them.

Transitional

The Transitional period (*c.*1760–70) was a short one, but it was very productive and some of the best pieces of the whole eighteenth century were made in those years. What were the main changes? A *commode* by Pierre Roussel of about 1770 may serve to illustrate. The whole shape has become rectilinear, the corners are canted and the legs have a gentle curve. The front is broken, with the centre part protruding and the *bombé* feature is not present. The marquetry is intricate, almost photographic, and the bronze-work is confined to small areas. The flamboyance of the Rococo has been passed by. Yet, despite changes such as straighter legs in chairs and desks, the older style did not entirely go away.

In this period there also appeared a great variety of small tables, whose descriptive names indicate their use: *table de toilette, table à jeux, table en auge* (work table). Some of them had mechanical devices for opening, locking and even changing their shape. At this time the roll-top writing desk, generally called *bureau à cylindre* was introduced. The type became popular when it was known that Louis XV had ordered one from his favourite *ébéniste*, Jean-François Oeben (*c.*1720–63), probably the greatest of all eighteenth-century

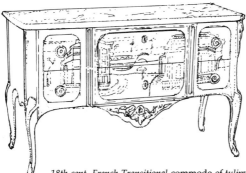

18th cent. French Transitional commode *of tulipwood, sycamore and marquetry of other woods, by Pierre Roussel, c.1770.*

French *ébénistes*. Oeben designed it and began making it in about 1760. This desk, which emerged as one of astonishing beauty and ingenuity, is now at Versailles again, and is the best known piece of eighteenth-century French furniture. Its value is impossible to assess. The desk is opened and closed by means of a revolving roll top, which is a quarter-cylinder made of slightly curved strips of wood closely linked together in line, which when motivated along curved grooving in the desk sides, either cover the desk's well or vanish into the carcase. This cylinder top was operated simply by turning the key, whereupon a hidden system of weights and pulleys raised it. The desk was not completed until 1769, over four years after the death of Oeben. The work was continued by Oeben's chief assistant Jean-Henri Riesener who in 1768 married Oeben's widow. Interestingly, the nine-year period of its making more or less spans the Transitional period, and in a sense its design resolves the contest between Rococo and the reaction against it.

The popularity of Sèvres porcelain plaques, medallions and panelling as alternatives or supplements to marquetry decoration gathered momentum during this period. By about 1760, the Sèvres factory had become a major competitor of Meissen, in Germany: this new outlet for its products, stimulated interest in decorative porcelain in furniture, clock faces, screens and so forth. Some *ébénistes* did not like it and would seldom use it, but others, notably Martin Carlin (*c.*1730–85), relished it as a decorative medium, and used it with great skill. A stock of panels and plaques would be ordered from Sèvres by a number of *ébénistes*, each piece being signed and dated by the factory. They would be stored in Paris and used when required; this means that a number of pieces of furniture with these plaques, medallions or panels are of slightly later date than the porcelain itself.

The drop-front *secrétaire* (*secrétaire à abattant*) was a most welcome development: it provided space to store papers rather than leaving

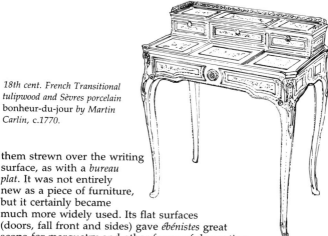

18th cent. French Transitional tulipwood and Sèvres porcelain bonheur-du-jour *by Martin Carlin,* c.1770.

them strewn over the writing surface, as with a *bureau plat*. It was not entirely new as a piece of furniture, but it certainly became much more widely used. Its flat surfaces (doors, fall front and sides) gave *ébénistes* great scope for marquetry and other forms of decoration.

The neo-classical ideas which emerged towards the end of the Transitional period as the prevailing styles for *ébénisterie* were not so successful with *menuiserie*, in which Rococo remained prominent, at least until the following (Louis XVI) period. Even so, in the opinion of this author, Louis XVI neo-classical chairs lack the grace and comfort of the Louis XV armchairs and settees.

Louis XVI

The last of the great eighteenth-century French styles can be divided into two phases: *c.*1770 to 1780, and *c.*1780 to 1795. The earlier was still full of extravagance, with classical forms following architectural principles but being heavily ornamented with gilt-bronze, with intricate and beautiful marquetry for surfaces persisting, and still with mechanical devices. Vast sums were still being paid out on furniture. Riesener is reported to have earned nearly one million *livres* over the years 1775–84 for royal pieces alone, while making a lot more for other clients as well. It was in the later phase that marked changes occurred.

In this second phase, France was at last feeling the effects of prolonged court extravagance (which had been aggravated by the wild excesses of Marie Antoinette) and equal profligacy among the nobility. Styles began to become simpler. More home-grown woods were employed instead of high-cost tropical varieties, although mahogany continued to be imported in great quantity as it was relatively inexpensive. Bronze mounts were whittled down and what were used declined in quality. Brass sometimes replaced gilt-bronze. Marquetry took second place in many pieces, behind plain wood, or less complicated parquetry, for panels, fronts,

18th cent. Louis XVI secrétaire à abattant in ebony, with Japanese black and gold lacquer panels, and gilt-bronze mounts, by J-H Riesener, c.1785.

sides. Though court furniture still maintained something of its traditional excellence right up to 1789, there is no doubt that the decline had set in elsewhere.

The Louis XVI period was nonetheless remarkable, and its star *ébéniste* was Riesener. Yet he was one only of over 200 maîtres working in Paris, to say nothing of the hundreds more assistants and apprentices. Pieces in fashion included roll-top desks (many both splendid and costly), *commodes*, *bureaux-plats*, and a range of smaller pieces designed for women, who still exerted great influence on furniture-making. Drop-front *secrétaires* were made in some quantity, many of them very impressive. *Bureaux-plats* tended to be rectangular rather than a mix of curved and straight planes and they carried less ornament. Some *commodes* had features additional to those of earlier periods, such as two or three large drawers below a frieze of three smaller drawers. While many *commodes* were break fronted, most were flat fronted, often with canted corners covered with mounts which were restrained and which accentuated the lines of the carcase, or fronted with pillars of one design or another. Legs were straight, turned, fluted or tapering, but the cabriole leg did not disappear altogether. A development of the *commode* that was much in demand was the *commode à encoignures*, which consisted of a central *commode* flanked by an arrangement of cupboards with shelves. There is one in the

Frick Collection in New York by Roger Lacroix (1728–99) in c.1770, which has been described as marking 'the triumph of classical over Rococo'.

Menuisiers continued to search for the ultimate in comfort and elegance in sofas, day-beds and chairs, although they were inevitably constrained by the dictates of classical lines. Upholstery thus became almost as important as the carving and decoration of the frame, and a variety of materials were used: silk in a rich array of colours, velvet, (gros point and petit point embroidery), moquette and damask. Chairs were also made with canework seats, sides, and/or backs, the cane attached to both front and back of the frame. Carved motifs included ribbon-work, cupid's bow and arrow, love-knots, acanthus leaves, laurel, and other designs produced to individual tastes. Woodwork was still gilded or painted, though much *menuiserie* appeared in plain wood, waxed or painted in clear lacquer.

Louis XVI chairs were in many respects different from earlier Louis XV chairs. Straight legs, tapering, sometimes fluted, reeded, or spiralled, and descending from cubes faced with rosettes on their outer sides, replaced cabriole legs. New types of chair back were the oval or medallion kind, first seen in about 1775, and also squarer backs, flanked by columns, with upholstered pads within the framework. In the 1780s, for the first time, some splat backs of the kind that had been enjoyed for decades in British homes began to appear in France, and some interesting designs were made.

Louis XVI armchairs usually had straight legs, and the arms were brought forward over the front legs. They rose upward and curved backwards into the back. Despite their graceful proportions, these chairs were somewhat rigid, like sixteenth- and seventeenth-century types, and did not have the relaxing properties of the splendid Louis XV *fauteuils*.

One of the chief chair-makers of the time was the eminent *menuisier* Georges Jacob (1739–1814), who was probably the first *menuisier* to use mahogany for chairs.

The last few years leading up to the Revolution of 1789 witnessed a headlong rush into national bankruptcy, headed by the court and the nobility which seemed unable to grasp the signs of impending trouble. Much skill was still being lavished on court furniture. Right up until the fall of the Bastille and beyond,

18th cent. French Louis XVI bergère *chair of c.1785–90, by Georges Jacob.*

Riesener and his colleagues made the most expensive pieces even though they were also finding it increasingly difficult to get paid. Outside court and aristocratic circles, some furniture-makers seemed to think the financial crisis was only a temporary one, and they also continued to oblige reckless clients. When, however, the king and queen had both perished on the guillotine in 1793, the old order had been swept away, and even the calendar changed, the full import of the Revolution hit the Paris workshops squarely. Demand for their work slumped and many craftsmen were reduced to poverty. Some hid away certain pieces to await better times. As the monarchy collapsed and the royal residences, like Versailles, became objects of national hatred, there followed a number of public sales of their furniture and other works of art. The contents of Versailles were itemized in some 17,000 lots and auctioned off. The National Assembly bought in some lots and put them in the Louvre but the principal buyers were English nobles and rich merchants who acquired shiploads of pieces at knock-down prices, incidentally helping to save them for posterity. The end had come to an unique period of furniture-making.

Directoire to late-nineteenth century

While the extravagances of the royal family and its circle were no longer possible, good-quality pieces were still in demand among the bourgeoisie. The king was dead, but the style named after him continued for a few more years, albeit in altered, less opulent form. The style that succeeded it came to be called the Directoire, after the government that followed the fall of Robespierre in 1794, and it lasted for only a few years. It resembled Louis XVI style but decoration was now less fine and less intricate, featuring new elements such as griffins, Roman fasces, cockades and sphinxes, the last included to celebrate Napoleon's campaign in Egypt. Economic difficulties persisted and they forced *ébénistes* to abandon veneers of rare woods in favour of solid woods, and to cut back enormously on marquetry. Chair legs, no longer cabriole or finely

Early 19th century French Empire style mahogany-framed settee.

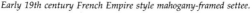

turned and tapered, became coarse, square sectioned, stubby sometimes, with large animal paw feet. Top rails were bulky and bent backwards. Frames were heavier, the shapes dreary and inartistic. During this period, imports of mahogany were temporarily halted, and one finds the stamps of famous *maîtres* on pieces made of humbler woods such as citrus.

The Directoire style gave way to Empire Style over the years. *c.*1804 to 1815, the years of Napoleon's imperial rule. Empire furniture was notable for the grafting of antique forms on to basic shapes, with little modification. Cornices, columns and pediments of classical design were 'plastered' on as ornament to cupboards, *commodes* and cabinets, but the grafts did not really blend. Dramatic effects were produced by contrasting dark red mahogany and glittering gilt ornament, or a brass imitation of it. Empire furniture was designed for show rather than comfort and, in the words of one furniture historian, 'it was a pathetic and theatrical apeing of Roman culture'.

New pieces to emerge in this heavy monumental style included glazed cabinets, break-front bookcases with lattice-work grilles, and various stands. Beds were ponderous, sleigh-like and claustrophobic. After the first decade of the nineteenth century, mahogany was sometimes rejected in favour of woods like beech (which could be dyed to look like rosewood but is much lighter in weight) and olive.

The monarchy was restored in 1815 in the person of Louis XVIII, a brother of Louis XVI. Emigré nobles began to return to Paris, and court and society started to live and behave as if nothing had happened since the 1780s. With this came a revival of interest in older eighteenth-century styles. Some craftsmen and dealers who had been active during the last years of Louis XVI's reign and who had hidden away much Louis XV and XVI furniture, now brought it out for sale. Many pieces were also brought back from abroad whence they had been taken by nobles who had fled from the Revolution. But it was only the returning nobles and their ilk who cared to buy pieces in these old styles, and prices were discouragingly low. A pair of *encoignures* with matching *commode*, made by Riesener, in the 1780s, fetched only about £100. In their first appearance they had cost several thousand pounds.

After a second revolution, in 1830, and the accession to the throne of Louis Philippe, who took an interest in architecture and furniture, there was once again a reversion to eighteenth-century styles, though by no means to the same degree as was to take place in the Second Empire of Bonaparte's nephew, Louis Napoleon (1852–70). *Ébénistes* began to reproduce these styles, sometimes slavishly, sometimes with original modifications, mixing them in a tasteful way. Some of the results were attractive, like the 1835 lady's writing table with *cartonnier* of drawers (see page 66) which clearly derives from the Louis XVI style.

The revival of national glory during the Second Empire helped

19th cent. French mahogany lady's writing table with shelf, inlaid with lime and sycamore, Paris, c.1835.

to generate a new upsurge of interest in the eighteenth century, and in earlier periods, too, as far back as *c.*1600. Pieces began to appear in several styles jumbled together. They were often very well made, using a variety of interesting woods, and veneering stood comparison with some of the best of eighteenth-century work. A number of highly skilled craftsmen took up the mantle of their eighteenth-century predecessors, and some, such as Louis-Auguste Beurdeley (1808–82), Henri Dasson (1825–96) and Alexandre-Georges Fourdinois (1799–1871) made names for work that was very good indeed. A fresh range of pieces in brass and tortoiseshell marquetry work appeared in the manner of André-Charles Boulle (see page 53), with the famous marquetry applied now to tables with violin-back-top, *commodes* with bombé fronts, cabinets with a large single door flanked by sets of curved shelves (like *commodes à encoignures*). Then there was a fashion for Louis XVI style, with cabinets inlaid with porcelain plaques (often though not always Sèvres) and covered with gilt-bronze mounts or brass stringing. At the same time, there was a great demand for seat furniture, like sofas, settees and armchairs, together with new types of seat, such as *confidantes* and *indiscrets* shaped to let two or three people sit together in such a way as to talk without being overheard and without appearing to be engaged in conversation. The chief characteristic of this and of other types of seat furniture was an excessive use of upholstery at the expense of the exposed framework. The status of upholsterer was raised above that of the cabinet-maker. There was also a flirtation with the Oriental, in the form of new chinoiserie, painted and lacquered decoration, and Chinese fretwork and leg forms. Then towards the end of Napoleon III's reign, there was a return to Renaissance designs, exemplified in such pieces as cupboards and double cupboards broadly in the styles of du Cerceau, Goujon and Sambin (see page

Mid-19th cent. French
*indiscret upholstered in
pink-red silk.*

Mid 19th cent. French walnut copy of
a Louis XV fauteuil, *with stuffed
seat, back and sides.*

Later 19th cent. French double
cupboard in ebony, *with gilt bronze
ornament, made in a mix of styles,
Baroque, neo-Classical and Empire
predominating.*

50), but having Baroque ornament encrusted with gilt-bronze figures and plaques, and in console tables mounted on carved and gilded figures.

In the later 1880s, there was a strong reaction against this 'messy' admixture of styles and ideas, and it heralded the Art Nouveau movement in France (see Appendix 1).

French provincial furniture: seventeenth to nineteenth centuries

French furniture between about 1660 and about 1795 is often described as if it were only the fine productions of the Paris workshops, but an enormous amount was made elsewhere in France during that period as well as before and after. There were considerable differences both between Parisian and provincial furniture, as well as between the furniture of the various provinces, and these differences in productions are reflected as much in the range of woods used as in areas of style.

Paris was a long way from cities like Bordeaux, Lyon, Marseilles or Lille, and few people in those and other cities and their provinces, knew anything about Parisian styles. Even the country nobility – a quite different class of people from the nobility in and near Paris – seldom visited the capital and knew little of its way of life. They filled their châteaux or *grandes maisons* with locally made articles in provincial styles and these styles were influenced by certain factors. Furniture was needed for a comfortable family life: there was little need to keep up with neighbours. Articles were limited to pieces such as beds, stools, *armoires*, chests, occasionally cabinets and *dressoirs*, and these were needed everywhere. They were made in varying styles in the different regions.

In the colder, northern areas, beds were usually the closed-in type: a simplified tester bed with hangings to keep out draughts. In the warmer south, in Provence for example, they were open and simple. The *armoire* (wardrobe) displayed regional variation in treatment, though basically it was the same piece, a two-doored, full-height cupboard for hanging clothes, with shelving. Most chairs had straw or rush seats, and simple slatted or plain panel backs. Better quality provincial chairs were fitted with cane seats and in some instances cane panels in the backs. Some of the woodwork, especially the front legs, might be carved. *Dressoirs* were fitted with differing numbers of shelves, others were open all round; some had boarded backs and sides, others had part of the shelving enclosed by small cupboard doors.

Taking one or two regions at random, simply to illustrate a few differences, Normandy furniture retained Gothic style decoration for a long time after Gothic had been superseded by Renaissance and Baroque in Paris and certain major cities. It continued to be made largely in oak, and it was fitted with brass hinges, handles and lock-plates. Furniture in Burgundy and in Gascony, though the two areas were a great distance apart, stuck to early seventeenth-century patterns long after not only Louis XIII (1610–

43), but also his son Louis XIV (1643–1715), had died. Alsace-Lorraine furniture was influenced by prevailing German and Swiss styles and some Alsatian cupboards were of good quality. Emphasis was on painting as the wood finish, rather than it being polished or inlaid. Walnut was the preferred wood, though the fruitwoods were also used widely. Metal fittings were often of polished steel or iron.

Paris-made furniture did not begin to have any marked influence elsewhere in France before the reign of Louis XV (1715–1774). For reasons not yet fully understood, the Louis XV style began to make a nation-wide impact from about 1730–40, and in some regions craftsmen continued to emulate Louis XV style and Transitional style up until the middle of the nineteenth century. The neo-classicism of the Louis XVI period, on the other hand, seems to have cut very little ice in many provinces, and at best was reflected in occasional classical details being superimposed on the basic curves and asymmetry of the Louis XV style.

Right, 17th cent. French Provincial upright cane-seat chair with loose cushion, and cane back, on scroll legs.

Below, 17th cent. French Provincial oak dresser (cupboard and shelves) from Gascony.
Below right, late 18th cent. cupboard on cupboard, painted in light blue, from Alsace.

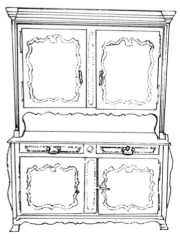

(5) GERMANY: SIXTEENTH TO NINETEENTH CENTURIES

The ideas of the Renaissance reached southern Germany from Italy sometime before they came to Germany north of the River Main. Numerous German artists, notably Albrecht Dürer (1471–1528) and Hans Holbein the Younger (1497–1543), had made lengthy visits to Italy in the early years of the sixteenth century, and had brought back new ideas which they incorporated into their work. One of the principal centres of southern German art was Nuremberg, and there, under the lead of the great craftsman Peter Flötner (d.1546), Renaissance ornamental forms were applied to German chests, cupboards, box seats, *dressoirs* and other pieces. Flötner's influence was immense, and before his death new styles of furniture making and decoration had been taken up throughout the south, and carried into the northern half. Yet the styles did not lead to new pieces; they were to come later.

Flötner was a designer as well as a craftsman, and he was probably the first to produce a book of designs, in a series of woodcuts which provided patterns for carvers and carpenters. One large cupboard in particular, made of oak and ash to his design in about 1540 at Nuremberg, clearly demonstrates his grasp of Italian ideas. Flötner's contemporaries adopted more and more of the Italian styles and German furniture became more architectural. A

Mid-16th cent. German Renaissance oak and ash cupboard made by Peter Flotner of Nuremburg (c.1540)

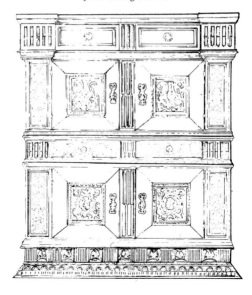

Mid-16th cent. German Renaissance slope-top writing desk with architectural decoration on back and sides.

writing desk of about 1554, for example, has a front that looks like the façade of a Renaissance cathedral, with Corinthian columns supporting pediments, and with highly decorative panelling. That it is actually a simple box desk seems almost to be an afterthought, for the slope starts midway down behind the elaborate façade. German craftsmen also began to specialize in inlay work, using boxwood, ebony, ivory, metal and marble. It was then that the great German tradition of fine marquetry began; two centuries later, German emigrant craftsmen were to work in Paris along with the French *ébénistes*, making superlative furniture in the eighteenth-century styles. It is no coincidence that Jean-François Oeben and Jean-Henri Riesener, the two leading *ébénistes* in Louis XV's reign were both of German descent.

In northern Germany, Renaissance styles were absorbed more slowly. Craftsmen continued to produce chests and cupboards, for example, in Gothic style well into the mid-sixteenth century, and the older form of construction of solid oak boarding persisted. Nonetheless, within this Gothic framework, individual wood-carving already began to reflect Italian ideas. In the mid-sixteenth century, northern German furniture also began to absorb Flemish Renaissance designs (see page 77), especially those of Cornelis Floris and his school at Antwerp. Before long, the fashion for *intarsia* from Italy (see page 42) reached northern Germany, where it enjoyed great popularity.

In the Thirty Years' War (1618–48), Catholic and Protestant German states suffered great misery and destruction as European powers fought their battles on German territory. Great palaces and modest houses suffered alike, and much furniture was destroyed. Creativity was choked in much the same way as it was in France during the wars of religion. Yet, before the Thirty Years' War was over, an architectural and craft revival was under way. Design books appeared in the 1640s. Workshops in several of the well-established centres in both southern and northern Germany were re-invigorated. Damaged palaces began to be restored and new Baroque style houses were built, giving German architects and cabinet-makers, especially of the Nuremberg, Frankfurt and, later, the Munich schools, splendid opportunities to exploit their skills to the full. This in turn, encouraged developments elsewhere. Walnut took over from oak. Design became more plastic and picturesque, with sharpened curves, stark profiling and elaborate foliate ornament.

This revival persisted in vigour and variety for the rest of the century – and beyond – and German furniture-makers maintained high standards of moulding work, planed and veneered. The Hamburg cupboard of the 1680s, illustrated below, is but one of many fine examples. Cupboards remained among the most frequently ordered pieces. Cornices show severe and top-heavy treatment. We see much of what is called auricular design, that is, a carved ornament with a distinctly fleshy, anatomical look, like a human ear, which was a development of scrollwork and which is found in other national styles. Tables followed the Baroque flashiness, often having legs in the form of caryatids supporting acanthus foliage, or shaped as dolphins, tail-upwards, joined near the bottom by a double-Y-shaped stretcher. Table tops were inlaid

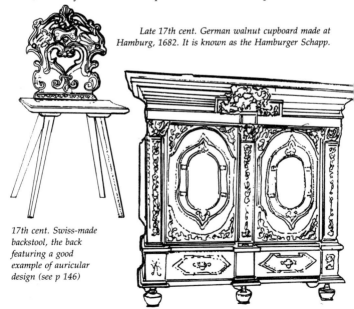

Late 17th cent. German walnut cupboard made at Hamburg, 1682. It is known as the Hamburger Schapp.

17th cent. Swiss-made backstool, the back featuring a good example of auricular design (see p 146)

Early 18th cent. German cembalo, lacquer-decorated on a white background, by Gerard Dagly, made for Frederick I of Prussia, c.1710.

with marble, all over or sometimes as an inner panel edged with marquetry. H.D. Sommer of Kunzelsau, who may have worked for a time in the Louvre workshops in Paris, under André-Charles Boulle (see page 53), used tortoiseshell and brass marquetry in the Boulle manner. The auricular decorative style was applied to legs, arms and top rails of backs of armchairs.

Lacquered furniture, meanwhile, also became fashionable, particularly in the styles developed by the great German japanning specialist, Gerhard Dagly (c.1650–1714), who was employed for years by the Brandenburg Court (later the Prussian Court). Dagly made very fine copies and adaptations of Oriental pieces such as cabinets and tables, and also constructed cases for clocks, harpsichords and other keyboard instruments. Lacquering was also applied extensively to wall decoration, in castles and houses, especially those on the Rhine, where whole rooms were panelled from top to bottom with lacquered boarding, and the furniture was often decorated to match. The taste for lacquer continued right through the rest of the seventeenth century and into the eighteenth.

To summarize the furniture of Germany in the eighteenth and nineteenth centuries in so short a space presents considerable difficulties. Then a land of numerous kingdoms and grand duchies, landgravates and margravates, and perforce including Austria in matters of architectural and decorative taste, each had its own particular versions of the prevailing styles – late Baroque, Rococo, neo-classical – that were dominated by France. Each maintained schools of craftsmen led by very gifted and very busy designers, and each ruler and his court seemed bent on spending profusely on building, decorating and furnishing palaces, great houses, castles, town halls and other public buildings and churches.

The main areas of manufacture were the traditional centres of Augsburg, Nuremberg, Mainz, Hamburg, Frankfurt, Würzburg, Berlin and Ansbach. All the craftsmen were to a large extent to be

Mid-18th cent. German three stage writing cabinet of walnut and other wood marquetry, with much emphasis on banding and chevron decoration. Made at Mainz.

guided by designer drawings which were widely and frequently issued in eighteenth-century Germany. The best known designers included François Cuvilliés (1695–1768), of Flemish descent, who worked first in Paris and then in southern Germany (including Bavaria) and began to publish designs in the 1730s; Georg von Knobelsdorff (1699–1753), of Berlin, who was chief architect to Frederick the Great of Prussia, and whose followers included Johann Michael Hoppenhaupt (1709–1755); Johann August Nahl; Joseph Effner, of Munich, chief architect at the Court of Bavaria, a follower of André-Charles Boulle and Charles Cressent (see page 55); and Abraham Roentgen (1711–93), founder of a workshop at Neuwied, on the Rhine, in 1750, whose son David was to work in Germany and France, and make pieces for Louis XVI, Frederick William II of Prussia and Catherine the Great of Russia.

German versions of the French styles were very distinctive. Some were fine imitations or modifications, others were somewhat overdone. Their Rococo furniture was on the whole more exuberant and undisciplined than French, with gay plastic motifs of figures, masks, Chinese dragons and so on. Chairs were sometimes very high backed with smooth splats, on large cabriole legs, sometimes with pronounced curving to the frame. By the mid-eighteenth century there was an abundance of pieces with lavish *rocaille* work and extravagant scrolling, and in many cases the most extraordinary shapes emerged, particularly in veneered

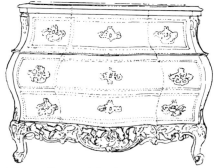

Mid-18th cent. German Rococo style bombé commode *of three drawers, with marble top and gilt bronze mounts.*

and marquetry- or parquetry-decorated commodes, where the *bombé* variety were often positively grotesque. We are considering the pieces made for the court and nobility in the German states. Burgher furniture followed French styles more closely, the Rococo reaching southern Germany in the early 1730s in a simplified form. Rococo prevailed throughout Germany into the 1780s: consoles, mirror frames, chairs, commodes, all were embellished with carvings of birds, flowers, garden tools, musical instruments, and gilding and painting were as popular as plain carved and polished wood. Pieces from Würzburg and Ansbach were often exceptionally ornate, decorated with the finest marquetry, and some splendid *trompe d'œil* work was also produced.

Most of the main workshops produced the conventional range of pieces, and two articles appear to have claimed special attention. One was the *bureau* cabinet, composed of a table with drawers, standing on heavy, curved legs with intricately carved knees, and

Early 18th cent. South German mahogany side table on four clustered column legs and wavy stretcher arrangement.

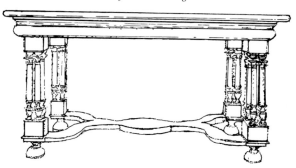

surmounted with a cabinet of immense elaboration. The other was the writing cabinet, distinct from the former by having a sloping front centre section between the cupboard top and the kneehole desk base.

By the last quarter of the eighteenth century, the Rococo had burned itself out in court circles, and the neo-classical style was replacing it. *Commodes*, writing tables, cupboards and chairs assumed more architectural proportions again, with straighter lines, though somewhat more ornamented than in France. One of the pioneers of the neo-classical style in Germany was David Roentgen (1741–1809), who produced very high quality marquetry within a neo-classical framework and established a reputation for being among the finest *ébénistes* in Europe, winning special praise from Catherine the Great of Russia, for whom he made, or directed the making of, some 200 items for her residences in Russia. He had also had the distinction of being made *maître* in Paris in 1780.

From about 1800, German craftsmen produced somewhat less elaborately decorated pieces in mahogany, poplar, ash and fruitwood, more in English Hepplewhite and Sheraton manner (see page 106), less in the Paris or Neuwied styles. Much of the furniture was light and graceful, and some of it was painted rather than polished or ornamented. After the Battle of Waterloo (1815), this lighter style became the forerunner of what is now known as the Biedermeier style. This stems from the name of a political caricature in a German newspaper, *Fliegende Blatter*, which catered for the tastes of the German middle classes. The style was based on a mix of French neo-classical forms with the domestic furniture of Britain, and other influences, and characteristic pieces included tables with curved legs, plain cupboards and chests of drawers, made from veneered wood. Decorative themes were treated in what may be described as a 'homely' fashion, with gilded metal ornament and carving simulated in paintwork. Many pieces were produced in mahogany. Sofas were upholstered with horsehair

19th cent. German Biedermeier style sofa, c.1820.

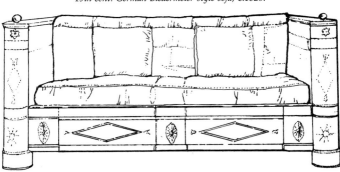

and covered with floral patterned calico and even rep. Some resembled the much earlier (fifteenth/sixteenth century) box beds, occasionally having Gothic tracery sides and panels. Secrétaires, cabinets and cylinder-top desks, were supremely functional, sometimes architectural (especially with cornices and pillars and sparsely decorated.)

In the 1840s and 1850s, Biedermeier went out of fashion among the upper classes, although it continued for a decade or so longer in the lower levels of society. It was replaced by the German neo-Gothic, but that did not survive and in the 1860s there was a return to other, much older styles, such as Rococo, Baroque and even Renaissance, but all these were jumbled and indeterminate like the mix of styles that affected America at much the same time. Worse, the German furniture industry began to graft what it conceived as 'Oriental' styles upon native furniture, which was neither one thing nor the other. This had two results. One was the enthusiastic espousal by many craftsmen of the Art Nouveau movement (see page 135); the other was the revival of interest in Biedermeier in the present century and its close study by some furniture historians.

(6) LOW COUNTRIES: SIXTEENTH TO NINETEENTH CENTURIES

The best late Gothic furniture (c.1300–c.1500) in the Low Countries was probably made in the workshops of Flanders, at places like Brussels, Bruges, Ghent and Antwerp, and it was here, probably before anywhere else, that the new styles of the Renaissance took root outside Italy. Flemish furniture clearly dating from the second half of the fifteenth century showed distinct architectural features, and in the first half of the sixteenth century Flemish styles took High Renaissance form under designers like Cornelis Bos and Cornelis Floris (1514–75). The latter was also a carver of exceptional skill who specialized in ornamental strapwork, scroll-work, grotesques, and applied motifs.

The leading influence in the last decades of the sixteenth century is generally recognized as having been Hans Vredemann de Vries (1527–1604), of Antwerp, an architect and painter. In about 1580, de Vries produced a book of ornamental designs and furniture, *Differents pourctraites de menuiserie*, which spread his ideas throughout the Low Countries and, eventually, Britain and Scandinavia. His son, Paul, continued this pioneering work with two further books of furniture design in the early seventeenth century. By this time there was a greater variety of pieces in the homes of wealthier people.

De Vries the Elder's book embraced designs for cupboards, tables, chairs, beds and chests, ornamented in bold Renaissance style and with a variety of new and often exciting motifs. They were essentially mannerist, featuring human and natural form. Carving was a vital element in the decoration of heavy wooden cabinets and chests, and biblical and classical scenes, geometric

Design for a tester bed by the Flemish designer, Hans Vredeman de Vries, c.1580.

devices and floral motifs sometimes completely overwhelmed their surfaces. De Vries specialized in, though he did not invent, the long draw table, sometimes wrongly called a refectory table. Two sections of the same thickness which together made up the same length as the top were drawn out and raised to the level of the top to produce a very long table. The top was supported on a joined frame with legs of turned, bulbous, baluster-type on ball or bun feet, linked by low, heavy, plain or ornate stretchers.

Chairs were upright and rigid, though leather seats and backs were fashionable for a long time. The leather upholstery was often elaborately tooled, as in Spanish chairs (see page 84), and not surprisingly when for much of the sixteenth century the Low Countries were part of Spain's dominions. One type of chair favoured in the later part of the century, and not owing anything to Spain, was the *caquetoire* ('gossiping' chair), thought to have been designed for women to relax in for conversation. It was usually made of oak, and had a tall, narrow carved back and widely splayed arms, with two upright supports for each arm. The back edge of the seat followed a wide arc or a semi-hexagon, to form a 'D-end' or a trapezoid-shaped seat.

Many Low Countries cupboards of the second half of the sixteenth century were very fine, some having carved front panels bearing X-shaped or parchemin panels, but with linenfold panelled sides.

For much of the seventeenth century, the Low Countries were divided into the United Provinces (Holland) in the north, which obtained their independence from Spain in 1609, and Flanders (much later, Belgium) in the south. The furniture of both areas was to be heavily influenced in the seventeenth century by the Baroque style from Italy, and the major centres of furniture-making were Amsterdam and the Hague, in Holland, and Antwerp and Brussels, in Flanders. For most of the seventeenth century both countries produced similar kinds of furniture – cabinets, cupboards (single and two-stage), bureaux, tables, chairs, stools and beds. Numerous paintings from Holland and Flanders of the time show in great detail just the sort of furniture that men and women had at home. It was in the decorative treatments that differences between Holland and Flanders began to emerge, largely though not entirely because the more southern craftsmen tended to stick to traditional styles while the freer northerners were stimulated to break new ground. To take the similarities first, both concentrated on the development of veneering, helped by the arrival in Netherlandish ports of new woods from the East and from South America, like rosewood, amboyna, as well as by growing expertise in the use of ebony, tortoiseshell, mother-of-pearl and brass. In their hands, the art of veneering developed to a very high degree, featuring dramatic contrasts between colours, in light and shade and in raised and flat surfaces.

In Holland, arcading was a dominant feature of the decorative carving on cupboards. These could be single-tiered, with one pair of doors, or two-tiered, with two pairs of doors. Both were usually about the same height. Cabinets had heavy raised panels with carving of flowers, fruit or birds on doors that were flanked by columns and surmounted by a cornice. This style gave way in the second half of the century to flatter, plainer but marvellously veneered surfaces to doors and sides, the contrasts effected by choice of woods, and by intricate floral marquetry, some so life-like that they looked like paintings, while the architectural framework faded into a secondary decorative role. This floral marquetry, some of the best of which came from the Amsterdam workshop of Jan van Mekeren (fl. c.1690–c.1735), was renowned throughout Europe, and the desire to copy and develop it spread to Britain and Germany, and even affected furniture in France (see colour section).

Late 16th cent. Dutch oak caquetoire (caqueteuse), with geometric design inlay.

*Early 17th cent. Flemish cabinet veneered in tortoiseshell and with painted panels
of classical scenes, and with ebony mouldings: made in Antwerp.*

Meanwhile, though Flanders was slower to break free of
convention, Antwerp craftsmen made an equally famous name for
their cabinets-on-stands with brass, tortoiseshell and ebony veneer
work, with inlaid drawer fronts bearing plaques of marble or other
materials, painted with religious scenes. Antwerp cabinets were
notable for dramatic surmounts of balustrading, free-standing
figures and pediments, perhaps recalling the work of the late
sixteenth-century French craftsmen led by Hugues Sambin, Jean
Goujon and others (see page 50). Antwerp craftsmen produced
cupboards of both single and two-stage type right to the end of the
century.

*Mid 17th cent. two-stage Dutch press cupboard of various woods, with arcading
at both levels.*

In the last decade of the seventeenth century, Low Countries furniture started to reflect new French styles. Part of this was due to the Revocation of the Edict of Nantes in 1685, when hundreds of French Protestant designers and craftsmen fled from their homeland and sought refuge in Holland and Germany and Britain, bringing with them many new ideas and the almost matchless skills with which to carry them out. One of the leading emigrants was Daniel Marot (1662–1752) who had been born in Paris. He got himself appointed architect to William, Prince of Orange (later, William III of England, Scotland and Ireland), and helped to introduce a new era of design and furniture into both Holland and Britain, in which architecture in a sense gave way to sculpture, and marquetry became more central to decoration, getting more complex and more beautifully executed, the patterns often reflecting the traditional Dutch love of flowers. Marot produced sets of engravings of designs for wide distribution among craftsmen. Some of these were inspired by Jean Berain (page 54).

In the later decades of the seventeenth century, Holland had also welcomed the new fashion for Oriental-style lacquered furniture. Dutch craftsmen were well placed to satisfy this taste because of Holland's extensive trading interests in the Far East, especially China and Japan. They imported completed pieces in some quantity, then brought in ready lacquered panels of a variety of sizes for insertion into home-crafted pieces of furniture, and also began to imitate the lacquerwork themselves, at first not very well, as surviving examples of crude European early lacquerwork show. One speciality in lacquered furniture was the cabinet with several small drawers in horizontal rows enclosed by doors or a fall front. Many of these are quite exquisite, and most museums in Europe have one or two examples, as do many historic houses that are open to the public.

The furniture of Holland and Flanders in the eighteenth century is usually described as having been dominated by French styles, especially the Rococo. While France certainly exerted a marked influence throughout nearly the whole of the century, we should not overlook two factors. One is the considerable native skill in design and craftsmanship of the Dutch and Flemish especially in the fields of carved woodwork, veneering and marquetry. The other is the interesting and well-documented link between Dutch and British craftsmanship and design, particularly in the first quarter of the century. Indeed, some authorities even now admit to problems in determining for certain whether a veneered bureau or a solid chair is of Dutch or English manufacture. An English strain was also found in some predominantly Rococo pieces. Take, for example, a chair of the mid-century, now in the Rijksmuseum: it has a Louis XV back and curving seat rail, and the top part of a conventional cabriole leg, but then the front legs terminate in English type claw and ball feet (see page 82). The Rococo reached its height in Holland and Flanders in the 1750s and 1760s: *commodes* (often veneered in burr-walnut, but only on the front); corner cupboards (with curvaceous mouldings); cupboards (the Flemish with much carving and extensive curved surfaces, and Dutch, with flat fronts, perhaps with canted or rolled corners); tea-tables (with low-level gallery and *bombé*-front single drawer).

Eventually, the reaction against Rococo reached Holland, and craftsmen began to produce neo-classical forms, some favouring the use of panels of Chinese lacquerwork, or imitations of it, such as on doors, secrétaire fronts and even on table tops. One interesting feature of some late eighteenth-century Dutch *commodes* in neo-classical form was tapering stub feet similar to those on the high thrones and stools of ancient Assyria (see page 12), though in inverted pyramid rather than conical form.

In the early nineteenth century, the Low Countries were completely dominated by France. Holland was a client state up to 1815, and the French Empire style prevailed. This was a pity, because Dutch and Flemish styles had had so much originality and attractiveness of their own for much of the eighteenth century, and of course before that. Even when the rightful Dutch monarchy was restored in 1815, the French styles nonetheless continued to swamp the market for some years, although Dutch preferred woods were employed, like walnut, maple and ash. In the 1830s, mechanical production methods affected the quality of pieces on a wide scale and drove the more traditional handskills into the background, though there was always custom for hand-made

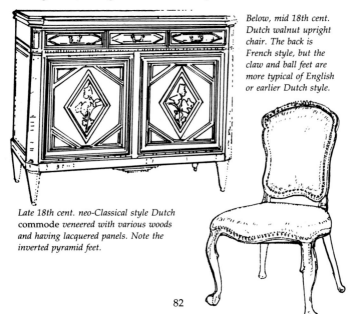

Below, mid 18th cent. Dutch walnut upright chair. The back is French style, but the claw and ball feet are more typical of English or earlier Dutch style.

Late 18th cent. neo-Classical style Dutch commode veneered with various woods and having lacquered panels. Note the inverted pyramid feet.

pieces. In the 1840s, as in several other European countries, there was a reversion to the styles of previous centuries, but mixing them up and in so doing creating eccentric and often unattractive furniture. Much the same has to be said for furniture made in Belgium, which was founded as a new kingdom in 1830 after breaking away from the restored Holland. It has been fashionable in recent years, because of the predominance of Brussels as a centre of the European Community, to question the contribution of Belgium to recent European history and civilization. It is gratifying to be able to reply that it was in Belgium, more than anywhere else, that the great Art Nouveau movement took root, in architecture externally and internally, and in decoration, furniture, ceramics, glass and textiles. It was not invented in Belgium, and its origins lay rather in the work and styles of William Morris (1834–96) and the English Arts and Crafts Movement, but it was in Brussels that its two leading exponents introduced it on a wide scale to Europe. They were the Belgian Baron Victor Horta (1861–1947), architect and designer, who studied in Paris and also in Brussels, and Henri van de Velde (1863–1957), the Belgian painter, born in Antwerp, who moved over to design and architecture in about 1890 (see page 135).

(7) SPAIN & PORTUGAL: SIXTEENTH TO NINETEENTH CENTURIES

It took centuries for the Christian kings in Spain to drive out the Moors. When the Moors were finally expelled in the 1490s, they left behind them ideas and culture that had become an integral part of Spanish life. These remained present to some degree for centuries, injecting their colourful exuberance and making Spanish furniture always interesting. When the new ideas of architecture and design arrived in north-eastern Spain from Renaissance Italy in the early sixteenth century, they were at first slow to spread. There was resistance in some areas where traditional skills were deeply rooted. But the results of unifying the kingdoms of Ferdinand of Aragon and Isabella of Castile and the empire-building they sponsored overseas in the New World and the Far East, and the riches these areas yielded to them, stimulated a dramatic economic revival. The Crown, the Church, the nobility and the wealthiest merchants – if no one else – began to spend money on new buildings and on decorating and furnishing them. In a new wave of furniture-making, the main woods used were walnut, chestnut and pine. In Catalonia, there were plentiful supplies of mulberry wood which was used in the solid form, and which resembled mahogany. By the middle of the century they began to use mahogany which came chiefly from Spain's new colonies in the West Indies and the Americas. This empire also provided silver from Peruvian mines and other precious metals and stones for inlays in furniture.

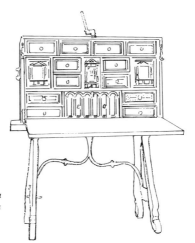

Late 16th cent. Spanish walnut vargueño with fall front down, on separate stand.

One of the earliest pieces of furniture to emerge in Spain at the end of the fifteenth century was the *vargueño*, or writing cabinet. It was a chest with a fall-front that could be used as a writing surface (and in some versions there was a lift-up lid as well). The chest was placed on a special stand, which had two horizontal pull-out supports (lopers) for the flap. The fall-front was often heavily decorated either with metalwork banding and ornate lockplates, keyhole escutcheons and spandrels, or inlaid with ivory, boxwood and other woods, sometimes in strongly Oriental patterns. The interior of the *vargueño* was a complex of drawers, rectangular or square, clustered round one or two small central cupboards, which were also decorated with Moorish or Renaissance motifs. The Renaissance element was displayed in architectural features such as columns and pediments round drawers and doors. There were iron handles on the sides for lifting. Later cabinets acquired two doors that hung vertically instead of a fall-front. In this form they were larger than the writing *vargueño*, and were used for holding valuables. In yet another form, there were two halves in one piece of furniture, a *vargueño* in the top placed upon a two- or four-doored cabinet. This was the forerunner of the later seventeenth-century and eighteenth-century writing cabinets, scrutoires and *secrétaires à abattant* of other countries. These two-part pieces were designed to balance on a mule. The portable nature of several of their types of chair made both chests and chairs suitable for travelling magistrates and other dignitaries who needed to reinforce their status when judging local cases, hearing catechisms, collecting rents and so forth.

Chairs became very common in early sixteenth-century Spain. Two main kinds graced most well-to-do houses, the hip joint type, known as the *sillón de cadera*, and the *sillón de fraileres* (monk's chair). The *sillón de cadera* was an X-shaped folding chair, and was

richly upholstered in velvet, with gold fringe
and braid, and the woodwork was often decorated with *mudéjar* (Gothic and Arabic) designs.
The *sillón de fraileres* also folded, but did so by
means of the front and back stretchers below
the seat being hinged in the centre,
allowing the chair to close up, like a
garden chair today. These were generally
leather-backed and leather-seated (see
right). Chairs that did not fold were
also made in quantity, particularly in
later years.

*16th cent. Spanish walnut and leather
upholstered upright chair.*

Cupboards assumed architectural proportions and were often
finely carved, even if sometimes more simply than in other
countries. There was widespread use of geometric mouldings for
doors, in some instances in the *mudéjar* 'zig-zag' pattern. Tables
were simple, virtually a variant of trestle tables, where the
supporting pairs of legs at each end slotted into the table top and
were held steady by iron hoop stretchers.

Portugal also produced fine furniture in similar styles, but with
clearly recognizable national features. Before the end of the
fifteenth century, Portuguese furniture was beginning to display
Oriental influence in the inlay-work on some pieces, made up from
materials such as ivory, precious
metals and stones, all acquired
during the colonial expansion of the
Portuguese that had begun in the
fifteenth century. Renaissance styles
affected Portuguese furniture as a
result of influences that came directly from Italy and France, by-
passing Spain. Chairs were of the
hip-joint type, beds were often
lacquered and decorated with gilt,
and chests were sometimes covered
with beautifully tooled leather.

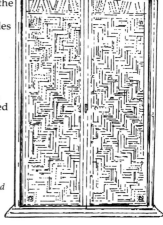

*Late 16th/early 17th cent. Spanish pinewood
cupboard decorated in* mudéjar *geometric
style.*

By the start of the seventeenth century, Spain dominated Europe. It had possessions in the Low Countries and Italy, and, until 1640, was united with Portugal. By then also, cracks were beginning to appear in its power and influence, the results of disastrous military and maritime adventures. Yet the monarchy and the nobility continued to live extravagantly, and did so throughout the century, spending prodigiously on buildings and furniture. The Baroque style had reached Spain in the last years of the sixteenth century, and it was to predominate for almost the whole of the seventeenth. In furniture, it was perhaps most widely reflected in seventeenth-century *vargueños*. Already popular among the nobility, *vargueños* now became the rage, and almost anyone who could afford to, ordered one, maybe two. Baroque style *vargueños* were of larger dimensions, were still dressed with architectural features, and were decorated with ivory pictorial plaques, and sometimes encrusted with jewels. Many had marquetry panels. Many were veneered with ebony and tortoiseshell and were fitted with gilt-bronze mounts. Some had elaborate galleries round the top. Two distinct types were fashionable, the *vargueño* proper with its fall-front, and the *papeleira*, with neither fall-front nor doors. Both stood on stands which themselves were elaborate, with a line of drawers or a deep curving apron, on bulb or swash-turned legs, with wavy or bobbin stretchers.

By the seventeenth century, chests had become unfashionable in Spain, except in country districts or small town homes. In their place came the dome-topped, leather- or velvet-covered trunk, with lots of brass or iron strapping, round-headed studding, mounts and lockplates. Cupboards continued to be made, some still featuring *mudéjar* moulding on doors. Long tables were supported on turned or columnar legs, and an interesting feature appeared under the table top in longer tables, a row of two or three carved-front shallow drawers in line in the apron.

From 1580 to 1640, Portugal and her colonial empire in the West

Late 16th cent. Spanish chest, from Catalonia.

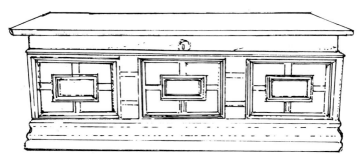

17th cent. Portuguese contador. The drawers are decorated with pierced brass strip on raised moulding.

and East were absorbed by Spain, and in that repressive period Portuguese furniture sacrificed some of its individuality and copied Spanish forms, in particular, upright and armchairs with leather upholstery. But when, in 1640, Portugal became independent once more, there was a revival in national architecture and design, which affected furniture that was developed by native craftsmen because foreign skills were not welcomed. Portugal's empire gave the home cabinet-makers opportunities to work with new and exotic woods such as jacaranda, pausanto, huang-mu and a variety of rosewoods (from the Far East). Portugal's revived involvement with its oriental colonies and with Far Eastern trading centres resulted in marked Oriental features in Portuguese furniture, and lacquerwork came into fashion. One of the most characteristic pieces of Portuguese furniture was the *contador*. This was like the *vargueño*, or more accurately the *papeleira*, as it did not have a fall front. It generally featured prominently raised panelling on the drawer fronts, heightened by brass or silver plaques. *Contadors* were often lacquered in gold, red and green. In the later part of the century, they were put on stands that were profusely carved

17th cent. Portuguese long table with elaborate moulding, bun and disc turnings, and fitted with metal ornament.

and decorated. The legs of some stands were extraordinarily 'over-turned' with bulbs, reels and swashes descending to flat, disc-like feet. This style of leg was also applied to tables (page 87). Cupboards were often two-storeyed, with sharply raised panel front faces.

In looking at Spain and Portugal in the seventeenth century, mention ought to be made of the styles of furniture in their overseas possessions. In grand houses of the governing and military classes in Spanish Peru, for example, the Baroque style was often blended with ancient Indian and Inca decorative treatments. Art and craft workshops were established in Mexico City and also in several South American centres, not only to encourage native skills but also to foster new design schemes and models that could be introduced back home in Europe.

By the early 1700s, much of the national vigour and originality of Spanish furniture craftsmanship had evaporated, and one could be forgiven for thinking one had seen some early eighteenth-century Spanish pieces somewhere else (France). Yet Spanish furniture still retained some of its barbarous native interpretation, and here and there old Moorish traits, which had affected architecture and furniture for so long were still detectable. Interestingly at this period, much furniture was still made in walnut, despite the easy accessibility of mahogany to Spain and the general trend towards using mahogany in most other European countries. The Rococo style became prominent in Spain soon after it had appeared in France, and there was a specialization in weird floral motifs in both carving and marquetry. Later on, there were also strong influences from Italy, particularly in the furniture that stemmed from the ideas of the Neapolitan designer, Matias Gasparini, who headed the Spanish royal workshops in Madrid from 1768.

Mid to late 18th cent. Spanish Rococo mahogany commode with gilt-bronze mounts, made under the direction of Gasparini.

The French-style *commode* replaced the *vargueño* and *papeleira* and became a major item of furniture in larger houses, made at first in solid woods, especially walnut, with carving and gilding, and then after Gasparini, with bold and gay marquetry. Spaniards also liked having small tables for many purposes and these appeared in a variety of French and English styles. Indeed, some English furniture designs were fashionable in several quarters throughout the century, partly as a result of Spain importing many English-made items. Chippendale-, and later on, Sheraton-style designs were adapted in Spanish chairs and carcase furniture, though these never eclipsed the dominance of what may be called Italo-French ideas, especially the seat furniture of Gasparini and his school, with its exaggerated scrolling and ornate aprons under the front seat rails.

Spanish provincial furniture clung to older and simpler forms, though towards the end of the eighteenth century, we do see these old forms merging with, rather than being replaced by, Rococo and, later, neo-classical designs, notably in chairs which, though still seventeenth-century in basic form, yet have Rococo or neo-classical carving on cresting rails, backs and arms, and some even were lacquered. One characteristic of Spanish furniture that survived in provincial pieces throughout the century was the taste for leather coverings on chests, seats and cabinets, the leather being embossed, coloured, gilded, studded and punctuated with wavy metal stringing. Portugal's long association with Britain led to the popularity of British furniture styles in Portugal throughout the eighteenth century. This may have been encouraged by the fact that, when the Portuguese princess Catherine of Braganza, married to Charles II of England and Scotland from 1661 to 1685, left England in the 1690s to go home, she is reported to have taken with her a shipload of English furniture, including chairs, tables,

Mid 18th cent. Spanish upholstered settee designed by Matias Gasparini for the Royal Palace in Madrid.

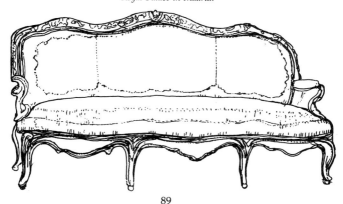

chests of drawers and so forth, some of them in the Dutch style. Chairs and beds are among the most representative pieces of Portuguese furniture of this period. In the first decades of the eighteenth century, chairs followed English and Dutch fashions but often had more sinuous and more intricate carving on crest and seat rails. As in Spain, they were often covered on back and seat with beautifully tooled leather. One characteristic of some Portuguese furniture of the Rococo period was the use of silver in place of gilt-bronze or brass for decorative mounts, handles and other features on case furniture and on tables. From quite early in the century, beds had no posts like the tester beds, and the emphasis was on the headboard which, once the Rococo style had arrived, presented fine opportunities for decoration. The day bed (see colour section), made of jacaranda wood, is in typical Portuguese Rococo style.

Above, mid-18th cent. Portuguese games table with interchangeable tops. The metal inlays and mounts are silver.

Right, a wonderful 18th cent. Spanish-Peruvian Rococo cupboard surmounted with a pierced carved cresting.

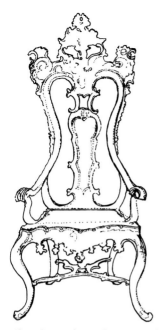

Above, later 18th cent. Portuguese colonial style armchair with tooled leather seat, made in Brazil, c.1770. Above right, early 18th cent. Spanish-Mexican upright chair with tooled leather seat and back panel, the back shape having pre-Columbian Mexican influence.

In the eighteenth century, both Spanish and Portuguese colonial furniture in the Americas began to take on more localized styles, while not altogether abandoning European models. Pieces appeared with most interesting mixtures of motifs. In South America, the Baroque style which had been superseded in Europe before the end of the first quarter, persisted almost to the end, and neo-classical is not seen until the late 1780s. Rococo, meanwhile, did reach the continent but not on any large scale. When Rococo motifs were employed, they were sometimes enormously exaggerated, as in a cupboard from Peru dating from the 1770s.

In Brazil, the heavier Portuguese designs persisted for a long time and were excessively ornamented. In Mexico, it was not unusual to find pieces revealing Aztec or other pre-Columbian features, such as the chair above. Chairs were still upholstered in tooled leather on back and seat in the Spanish late mediaeval and Renaissance manner.

The involvement of both Spain and Portugal in the Napoleonic Wars in the first two decades of the nineteenth century had serious social and economic consequences. Even after the defeat of Napoleon in 1815, there was unrest, repression and then civil war

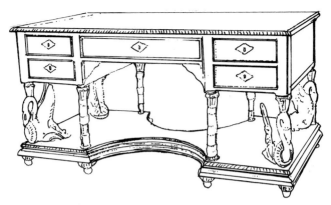

Early 19th cent. Spanish 'Fernandino' style mahogany desk on swan supports.

in both countries during the next half century. For the first years of the nineteenth century, the furniture of both Spain and Portugal tended to continue in the French Empire style of the early nineteenth century. Most pieces of Spanish manufacture were of mahogany, with much gilt bronze and heavily gilded arms, legs, supports and other decorative features. Spanish furniture made in the period *c.*1815 to 1835 is sometimes called Fernandino style, after the restored King Ferdinand VII (1814–33), and this style was replaced in the late 1830s by a strange and reactionary reversion to a quasi-Baroque style, sometimes called Isabellino, after Ferdinand's successor Isabella II (1833–68). Isabellino was marked by excessive carving, gilding and upholstery, some of the carved superstructure on pieces looking quite absurd. There are pieces in the Museo de Artes Decorativos in Madrid which almost defy description. Most of this weird furniture was made for the royal family and the nobility, while among the lower classes furniture continued to be simple and conventional, hardly differing from that of the previous century.

After recovering from war devastation, Portugal produced furniture in French neo-classical and Empire styles. In the 1820s we see also an injection of English taste, particularly in major towns, and in the capital, Lisbon which had been devastated by an earthquake in 1755 and where some of the rebuilding work was planned and designed by British architects, including Robert Adam. Designs in Portugal drew much from Thomas Sheraton and his contemporaries, and there was an interest in the English Regency style. In the 1830s and 1840s, Portugal, like Spain, adopted a neo-Baroque fashion, and though it is of course a matter of personal opinion, the Portuguese productions were on the whole more pleasing than the Spanish.

(8) BRITAIN: SIXTEENTH TO NINETEENTH CENTURIES

England and Scotland were late to receive and slow to accept new Renaissance styles, especially outside London where craftsmen were – and continued to be right into the nineteenth century – extraordinarily conservative. Although carving was sometimes of a high quality – English linenfold, for example, was particularly fine – carpentry and joinery were both poor compared with Italian, German and Flemish work. Joinery had been practised in Britain as far back as the fourteenth century but it was not until the later sixteenth century that joiners and carvers formed themselves into a guild, which received its charter in 1570–71. That is not to say good joinery was not produced before, but the recognition of the guild gave considerable encouragement to a craft that had been hampered by being the 'poor relation' of the carpenters' guild. From then on, joined furniture advanced rapidly, fast replacing boarded pieces, and by the end of the century, dovetailing was beginning to be used for joints. While the number of pieces of joined furniture which one can be fairly sure belong to the later sixteenth century is small, the quality is often very good. Contemporary inlay work, on the other hand, was still crude and of limited adventurousness: patterns were generally confined to simpler geometric designs, squares, lozenges, and basic floral motifs.

The growing wealth of the new middle class in England and Scotland, and to a lesser extent in Wales in the last years of the sixteenth century, provided opportunities for more experiment among craftsmen and Italian, French and Flemish styles began to be popular, though these influences were tempered by an

Mid to late 16th cent. English oak joined armchair, with linenfold panels. The panels are missing from under the arms and between the seat and side stretchers.

undercurrent of simplicity which if anything became more pronounced as England and Scotland began to lean towards Puritan ideals. As elsewhere in Europe, the range of pieces made was still small and consisted chiefly of chairs (backstools, armchairs, *caquetoires* and X-shaped chairs), benches and settles, folding, trestle and withdrawing tables, court cup-boards, press cupboards, livery cupboards, boarded and joined chests, tester beds and writing boxes. Much of this furniture was made in oak, but other woods were employed, including the fruitwoods (among them apple, pear and cherry), ash, elm and chestnut.

Some surviving pieces of sixteenth-century furniture have a rich patina, the result of vigorous and frequent waxing and polishing over the years, and an effect that cannot be faked. It seems that even in the sixteenth century English wood craftsmen were experimenting with polishes that have not altered much since. Boiled linseed oil rubbed into wood in its natural state accentuated the grain. The sixteenth-century Continental fashion for painting and gilding furniture was not followed in England to any great extent at the time.

One of the pieces on which much carving skill was applied was the tester bed, an interesting part-restored example of which is shown in the colour section. Tester beds were not exclusive to Britain, but some good sixteenth-century examples have survived, wholly or in part, and they were decorated with splendid woodcarving on their posts, headboard(s) and testers. Most tester beds were fitted with curtains all round, to keep out draughts. At this time, and later, too, the bedroom was occupied probably for longer each day than any other room, particularly in the winter months. Numerous pictures and engravings of the period show kings, princes and other royalty, receiving all kinds of visitors while in bed. In many households, families spent long hours in the master's bedroom and some even took meals there. Many bedrooms were equipped with livery cupboards for storing food and drink for the evening and, if needed, during the night.

Another piece of furniture which was often the subject of profuse carving was the cup-board (as distinguished from the cupboard), the open display shelf unit of two or three tiers. These are called court cup-boards ('court' being the French for 'short'), almost certainly because their height is below average eye level, so that the display on the top can easily be laid out and seen.

The conservatism of British furniture craftsmen continued to prevail in the first half of the seventeenth century. Many of the more luxurious pieces which can reliably be dated to between c.1600 and c.1660 were either made abroad and imported, or made either at home by craftsmen who had studied abroad, or by foreign craftsmen working in Britain. In a sense, this means that up to the time of Charles II's restoration in 1660, furniture falls into two distinct kinds, the 'foreign' pieces (many of which had a Baroque character) and the good, old-fashioned home products, which

17th cent. English oak small chest with arcaded front surmounted by knulling decorated top rail.

were often no more than refinements or improvements upon what the makers' fathers or grandfathers had been making in Tudor times. There was an upsurge in making back-stools (the seventeenth-century term for upright chairs without arms), which in the previous century had been little more than a stool fitted with a single narrow vertical stile to support the back, or a line or arc of narrow uprights topped by a rail. Before long, distinctive regional types evolved (splendidly described and catalogued by Dr Bill Cotton in a recent book, *The Regional Chair*). Among the better known of these regional chairs was the Yorkshire-Derbyshire type, made of oak, a typical one being carved on its arcaded cresting rail, and having turned baluster front legs and a solid flat or dished wooden seat. Another type had a simple padded back covered

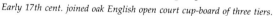

Early 17th cent. joined oak English open court cup-board of three tiers.

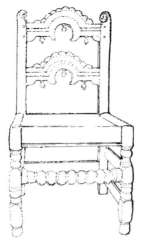

Early to mid 17th cent.
Yorkshire or Derbyshire
upright chair with solid
seat and bobbin-turned
front stretcher.

with embroidered cloth or plain leather, an overstuffed and covered seat and narrow legs which could be bobbin-turned, baluster-turned, columnar or of square section. Another interesting chair was the 'thrown' chair ('thrown' meaning 'turned'). This was made by a separate branch of the woodcraft trade, the turner, who specialized in chairs (and also made turned parts for other pieces) and whose guild, the London Turners' Company, was given its charter in 1604. The 'thrown' chair was made of units shaped by turning on a pole lathe. Woods were ash, elm, yew, beech, but seldom oak. Some of these chairs were triangular in plan (see colour section).

Other pieces of furniture made in growing quantities and featuring more interesting designs and carvings were gateleg tables (especially with two flaps), side tables and, by the 1640s, the earliest English chests of drawers. These last-named had evolved from plain carved and panelled chests where (first) the chest part acquired a pair of drawers underneath, then a pair in line, with another double-width drawer under that. By the 1600s, the first dovetailed joints were being employed to join two boards together at right angles, across the end-grain. The method was used in the construction of drawers, boxes and small cupboards. Dovetails began by having both tongues visible at the joint, then having one lapped so as to obscure it. The latter was a stronger join. In the provinces it was usual to strengthen dovetails by ramming a nail through a tongue when it was pressed into the slot, but in higher-quality joints the practice was abandoned when superior glues, better techniques and better woods arrived. Before 1650 the first chests of drawers, using dovetails, were being made.

Early 18th cent. Indian painting of a maid making a canopied bed, which stands on bell shaped feet. (See page 17)

1st cent. AD Roman couch from Boscoreale (restored). (See page 34)

Left, 7th/8th cent. AD MS picture of an opened cupboard with shelves of books, a stool, a footstool and a small table: from the Codex Amiatinus, 689–716 AD.

Below left, late 16th/Early 17th cent. French walnut Baroque style double cupboard, in the style of du Cerceau. (See page 50)

Opposite above, this Louis XV commode was made by Antoine Gaudreaux (1680–1751), based on the design of the Slodtz Brothers (see drawing on page 57), in c. 1739.

Below, Louis XV bombé commode made and stamped by Pierre Roussel (1723–82). (See page 57)

Above, the Bureau du Roi *made for Louis XV between 1760 and 1769. Designed and begun by J-F Oeben, completed by J-H Riesener, the mounts were by Duplessis and Hervieux. Probably the most famous piece of furniture in the world. (See page 60)*

Right, early 18th cent. Low Countries double chest of drawers of oak, lacquered in red and gold on black in imitation of red tortoiseshell.

Late 17th cent. Dutch marquetry-decorated cabinet on stand by van Mekeren of Amsterdam. (See page 79)

Mid-18th cent. Portuguese Rococo-style jacaranda wood day-bed with tooled leather pallet. (See page 90)

Above, early to mid-17th cent. English oak tester bed. (See page 94)

Right, early to mid-17th cent. English ash and elm "thrown" armchair. (See page 96)

Left, late 17th cent. English oak chest of drawers veneered with walnut and other woods, and ornamented with fruitwood mouldings.

Below, mid-18th cent. English drop-leaf table with Cuban mahogany top and oak frame on mahogany legs.

17th cent. Scandinavian oak trestle table.

19th cent. Swedish birchwood oval table on pedestal support. (See page 117)

Cabinet-making as a skill had been known in Britain from the end of the sixteenth century, though it was practised not by native craftsmen but by German and Flemish immigrant craftsmen who set up workshops in several places, notably Southwark, in London, and Norwich. These men were often called skrynemakers, from the Latin *scrinium*, a chest, and in some specialists' opinion they were the legitimate ancestors of the great eighteenth-century English cabinet-makers.

The restoration of Charles II heralded new times, which were to break away from the mood of asceticism accompanying the cutback in spending in the Commonwealth period. This new age was reflected in furniture. Walnut, which had already been used extensively for furniture in Europe for some time, now came into fashion in England and it continued to be the favoured material of English furniture-makers for over half a century. Solid walnut began to replace oak for chairs, day-beds and some tables. It was used in veneer form on oak or other woods for cabinet-making. The natural beauty of its grain and its mellow colour appealed to a new and colourful age, and, in skilled hands, it lent itself to the most complex kinds of decoration. Typical walnut pieces that have survived from the period in some quantity include chairs, *bureaux*, chests of drawers, chests-on-stands and chests-on-chests, side tables, centre tables, cabinets, bookcases, and long-case clocks.

Though dominant, walnut was not the only material for solid furniture making: oak was not abandoned, while ash, beech, elm, pine and various fruitwoods were widely used in the country

Late 16th cent. 'Nonsuch' chest inlaid with light coloured woods. Architectural scenes were a feature in these chests, which were made usually by emigrant German craftsmen in England.

districts. Additionally, the taste for decorating wood with coatings became fashionable as alternatives to waxing. One of these was gilding, normally done by first applying to the carved surface a paste of fine chalk mixed with slim parchment scrapings (size). The result was called gesso, and it was rubbed smooth and then gilded with gold leaf. Gesso could be applied to plain surfaces as well, though not always with success. Another coating was lacquer-work, already widely used on the continent. At first, lacquering was confined to case furniture like cabinets and some chests of drawers, and to begin with finished articles were imported from the Far East (India, China and Japan). They were mainly coloured in black and gold. Later, importers brought in shipments of panels of various sizes already lacquered, for craftsmen to assemble or alter to make finished pieces. Finally, by about 1680, craftsmen had begun to copy lacquering techniques, introducing fresh colours such as red, green and yellow. Books on varnishing and lacquering began to appear: one of the most popular was John Stalker and George Parker's *Treatise of Japanning and Varnishing*, 1688. The vogue for lacquerwork became popular very swiftly and resulted in much inferior work being produced to meet demand. After cabinets with two doors enclosing rows of drawers, the technique was applied to tables, some types of chair, and small fall-front desks. The decorative patterns were often beautiful, though not excessively imaginative, and were generally confined to country scenes with birds, flowers, houses, small bridges, trees, all summed up in the word chinoiserie.

The other very important and popular decorative treatment was veneering. Crude and simple inlay work of coloured woods cut and arranged to make floral or geometrical patterns had been produced in the late sixteenth and early seventeenth centuries, but it was not till the 1670s that veneering (or 'faneering' as it was originally de-scribed because of the technique of cutting the wood slices across the grain to produce a fan-like appearance) really took off in Britain. Veneering was generally ornamented in some way, with marquetry, oystering, parquetry, quartering, feather banding and stringing. Marquetry was a major advance on inlay and was different. Patterns of contrasting light and dark coloured woods were applied to surfaces of case furniture.

Early 18th cent. English Queen Anne style beechwood upright chair on cabriole legs, with stretchers, painted black and other colours to look like lacquerwork.

Patterns and their backgrounds were often cut together from the contrasting woods and glued together on the carcase. Slanting the veneer cutting saw produced a sloped edge to ensure a tight fit. Fashionable patterns included flowers, birds, foliage, seaweed-like effects, and arabesques. The earlier marquetry in Britain was directly influenced by Dutch styles.

One of the very attractive marquetry design styles was oyster veneer, applied to cabinet doors and drawer fronts, table tops and chests of drawers. This veneer pattern is cut from small branches and placed down together to create a pattern resembling a grouping of oval and round oysters. Woods used for oyster veneering included laburnum (with its yellowish hue and light brown streaks), olivewood and kingwood. Sometimes these patterns were heightened by boxwood stringing in straight lines or curving lines, usually forming symmetrical patterns. Another form of decorative veneering is parquetry, which was in its infancy in Britain in the late seventeenth century. Here, a range of geometrical patterns was formed by contrasting shades of veneer. Quarter-veneering was achieved by cutting four pieces of identically figured veneer and laying them side by side in a square or rectangle. It was used for drawer fronts, chest tops, table tops, cabinet fall fronts and so forth. Feathering was produced by cutting very thin strips of wood diagonally across the grain running diagonally, then placing them along the edge of another veneer; sometimes two opposing diagonals were placed together to form a chevron patterned border. This is called herringbone banding. Stringing consisted of a line of inlay of satinwood, boxwood or purplewood, or ebony, used like wire to make a decorative border. One piece of furniture in the later seventeenth century that underwent much development was the chair. The loosely called Charles II type featured a number of new designs, such as cane seating, cane backs in long, narrow panels held between solid upright muntins which were flanked on either side by baluster-

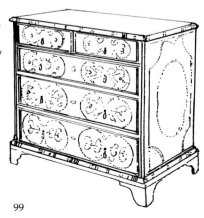

Early 18th cent. English William & Mary style small chest of drawers of oak with oyster veneer decoration of laburnum wood, and with marquetry of other woods.

Early 18th cent. English William & Mary style walnut chest of drawers on stand, the drawer fronts edged with herring-bone inlay.

turned or twist-turned supports, surmounted with elaborately carved cresting rails, carved stretchers between the front legs, carved seat rails and turned, shaped and carved legs. With the accession of William III and Mary II in 1688, chairs began to incorporate C- and S- scroll motifs, and X-shaped stretchers were joined to all four legs in a wavy X-shape. The first cabriole legs appeared, to be greatly developed in the first half of the next century.

The eighteenth century opened with new ideas in the walnut furniture made in England, largely through the influence of Daniel Marot (1663–1752), the French-born 'designer-general' to William of Orange (later William III). He had a hand in almost every aspect of architecture, decoration and furnishing: he laid out gardens, he designed buildings, he sketched schemes for interior decoration, he produced drawings for furniture and clocks, and even suggested motifs and shapes for ceramics. His designs in many fields were published mainly in Holland but they were also sold in England, and for a time in France, too. His influence had already been strong in Holland, and was to remain so for many years, and this may be one of the reasons why there are still difficulties encountered in distinguishing between English-made and Dutch-made pieces during this period, without documentary evidence of origin. He introduced new furniture designs with decorative outlines, such as pediments, single or double domes, broken and unbroken arches, scrolls and so forth. Doors for wardrobes and early bureau-cabinets and bureau-bookcases were panelled rather than flat-veneered. Silvered glazing was often used in the doors or top cupboards of bureau-cabinets. Cabinet-makers began increasingly to use cross-banding, (cross-grained wood to give contrast) on veneered surfaces. Mirrors now appeared in many rooms of houses, where they filled awkward spaces between windows or surmounted heavy mantelpieces. Carving and gilding of mirror frames were not new, but were employed much more profusely. Gilt decor was also applied to chairs, tables, stools and consoles.

William III died in 1702 and was succeeded by his sister-in-law Anne, but the style now called Queen Anne had already begun, and was to continue after her death in 1714, when George I succeeded her. Many Queen Anne pieces were straight walnut veneered, with or without inlay or marquetry, on oak or pine carcases. Mouldings were more interesting and varied, and applied on curved surfaces, flat surfaces and even in sculptural form. Some of the new pieces had novel shapes, like fold-over card-tables with swing-out bowls for money and dished circles at the edges for candlesticks. Bureau-cabinets and bureau-bookcases with doors in the top stage, single or double, depending on the width of the piece, had drop fronts in the middle, covering small drawers in rows, pigeon holes above or beside them, secret compartments, and sliding top well, and below this section drawers set in chest of drawers style.

Late 17th cent. English looking glass in gilded frame, carved in the manner of Grinling Gibbons, c.1680.

From about 1720 it became more difficult to get hold of walnut for furniture-making. Embargoes were placed on its import from Europe because of shortages there, and stocks of native wood were beginning to run out. Cabinet-makers looked further afield and found a darker and closer-grained variety in the American Colonies. They also increased their purchases of mahogany from Spain and America. It was still relatively inexpensive. It was worm-resistant and it was a lovely wood to carve. From about 1740 a particularly rich variety became available from Cuba. It was not to be long before walnut receded into second place as the dominant wood for cabinet-making among people of wealth. In poorer homes and country districts traditional preferences for oak, pine and fruitwood persisted.

The attractive qualities of mahogany, together with the growing prevalence of French styles throughout Europe, led to changes in English furniture styles, from about 1740 onwards, though Britain never took enthusiastically to the wilder manifestations of the Rococo. A summary of the story of British furniture in the later eighteenth century can reasonably be made by looking at the designs and works of the leading designers, especially those who dominated the period – Thomas Chippendale (1718–79), George Hepplewhite (d.1786) and Thomas Sheraton (1751–1806). The work of these men well illustrates the heights to which British furniture design rose in the period, but in considering these 'giants' we must not overlook the work of equally fine contemporary designers and craftsmen, notably William Kent, William Vile, John Cobb, Ince and Mayhew, and John Linnell, and not forgetting the creative work of great architects who influenced furniture, none more perhaps than Robert Adam (1728–92).

Thomas Chippendale was born at Otley in Yorkshire in 1718. He came to London in about 1748, after several years' work in Yorkshire as cabinet-maker, and five years later he moved to St Martin's Lane where he remained until his death in 1779. St Martin's Lane was a sound choice for it was an area noted for artists' residences (Reynolds and Thornhill both had houses there), and furniture-makers had already started to set up nearby. In 1754, Chippendale published a book of furniture designs, *The Gentleman and Cabinet-Maker's Director* (usually shortened these days to the *Director*). It was a success, a reprint followed the next year, and between 1759 and 1762 a third impression appeared, this time in serial parts, larger and with much revision. The *Director* was to have a big effect on English styles for years.

At this time, some English furniture-makers were dabbling with Rococo designs, and also with Chinese style ideas (loosely called chinoiserie) and revived Gothic styles, the latter championed by Horace Walpole at his unusual home, Strawberry Hill, Twickenham. Chippendale produced designs in all these styles, stamping some of them with individual ideas of his own. He adorned his furniture with exquisite fretwork in Chinese taste,

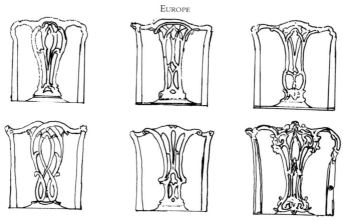

Six chair-backs from Chippendale's Director, *1762 edn.*

using it for edging tables, doors of cabinets and bed canopies. He designed and made Gothic style chairs, and he also produced his own ideas of Rococo, favouring the use of ribbonwork, fruit swags and exaggerated cabriole legs, in combination with shell ornament. Principal pieces were chests of drawers, sofas, china cabinets, writing tables and chairs. Some of his ideas were over-elaborate, as designs in the *Director* show, but pieces following the essential forms of his design but without the refinements could be made by ordinary country joiners and cabinet-makers as well as lesser London craftsmen. This was the origin of so much furniture that is described as Country Chippendale today. It was copied in his life-time and has been ever since.

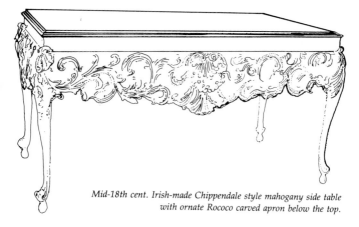

Mid-18th cent. Irish-made Chippendale style mahogany side table with ornate Rococo carved apron below the top.

Mid-18th cent. English mahogany library table made by Chippendale for Nostell Priory, 1767.

As far as the designs in the *Director* are concerned, there has long been argument as to how many were actually his idea, and how many were those of colleagues for whom he volunteered to publish. But the book established his reputation, and it seems that his own work as cabinet-maker was markedly finer after the publication than before! How much he made himself will never be properly known, and surviving bills made out by him to purchasers are probably the only safe means of attribution. The owner of Nostell Priory was billed by him for a magnificent library table for £72.10s., and there are a number of similar accounts. He also employed designers, marqueters, carvers and joiners in his workshops and his sons also worked for him. But in the end he was but one of many proprietors of cabinet-making businesses. After the arrival of Robert Adam on the architectural and interior design scene in the 1760s, Chippendale had to take a back seat, though not for long, for he was quick to accept commissions to produce designs and make furniture in the neo-classical style being pioneered by Adam. It used to be thought that Adam ordered designs from Chippendale for furniture to fit into the overall decorative interiors he originated for a variety of houses, but we know now that most of the time Chippendale dealt directly with the building owners. It is difficult to be precise about what if any pieces of furniture Chippendale actually invented, for the designs published in the *Director* were much more a catalogue of what was available than what was an innovation. Probably everything had been thought of before, but the book for the first time spread the possibilities around among owners, designers and makers alike, altogether in one volume. Pieces that were relatively new on the scene included shaving tables, basin stands, tea kettle stands, library tables, bookcases (large and glazed-doored), china cupboards and shelves, chimney pieces, girandoles, cisterns, wine coolers, and the book also contained varieties of new types of old established furniture, such as beds, mirrors, picture frames, chairs, sofas and chests of drawers. We must not forget, either, that his contemporaries mentioned above (page 102) and others were producing designs and making pieces of the same and similar kinds, of which they may in part have been originators. Ince and Mayhew, for example, produced a book *The Universal System of Household Furnishing* which contained upwards of 300 designs 'in the most elegant taste'. It was published in the same period as Chippendale's third edition of the *Director*, and there are numerous differences in general and in particular.

Robert Adam was born at Kirkcaldy in Scotland in 1728. He was the son of the architect William Adam (1689–1748) and studied under him in Edinburgh. In 1753 he went to Italy to enlarge his knowledge of classical and European architecture, and spent much time studying the results of the discoveries at Pompeii and Herculaneum which had recently been excavated. He met many leading Italian architects and designers, and in particular the influential architect and artist Giovanni Battista Piranesi (1720–78) who was largely responsible for the Classical Revival in Italy.

When he came home, Adam set up a practice in London in 1758 with his brother James, also an architect, and over the next thirty or so years he introduced a whole series of new architectural ideas which resulted in a classical revival in British building design and interior decoration. Adam understood the value of relating interiors to exteriors, and his concepts of interior decoration rested on ancient Greek and Roman motifs, characterized by the use of the oval, and featuring strings of flowers, shell ornament, scrolls

Early 19th cent. English elmwood country Chippendale style armchair, with solid seat.

of foliage and painted panels in low relief. He produced a huge quantity of drawings (many of which can be seen at Sir John Soane's Museum in Lincoln's Inn Fields in London) and many were designs for furniture, invariably drawn as an integral part of overall schemes of interior decoration.

The Adam brothers won numerous commissions for designing new houses and decorating them inside and outside, and also for renovating or improving existing houses and public buildings. In this process they commissioned new furniture from leading cabinet-makers.

Robert Adam's furniture styles were departures from prevailing Georgian tastes, and included chairs with straight, tapering, turned legs, fluted, reeded or plain. Chair-backs were often oval, dispensing with the cresting rail. Symmetry, order and formality predominated. Here and there Adam showed some influences from French styles, but nothing could displace his own individuality, which was to dominate the architectural and decorative scene to the end of the eighteenth century.

The next furniture-maker who was also an originator and designer was George Hepplewhite (d.1786), who is really something of a mystery. We do not know when he was born but he

Six chair-backs from Hepplewhite's Guide, *1788. Four are shield-backs.*

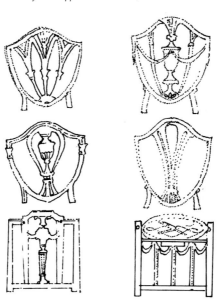

Late 18th cent. English mahogany Hepplewhite design bow-fronted sideboard.

learned cabinet-making in Lancashire and started to design and make furniture in London. Nothing known to have been made by him has survived, and though he produced a book similar to the *Director*, it was not published until two years after his death (1786) by his widow. The book, *The Cabinet-Maker and Upholsterer's Guide*, gave him a fame he had never had while he was alive. The book was, so far as we know, the first of its kind since the *Director* and the Ince and Mayhew work, and it, too, had nearly 300 drawings. Many of Hepplewhite's designs reflect the influence of Robert Adam and many were intended to be made in mahogany, with inlay, chiefly of satinwood, or marquetry loosely in the French manner. Like Chippendale, Hepplewhite was particularly interested in chair-backs and the *Guide* gives us an idea of the variety he designed in his career. The most familiar of the Hepplewhite chair-backs is the shield-back with a variety of splats inside. One popular range incorporated the Prince of Wales ostrich feathers motif in various forms. Many Hepplewhite chairs have square tapering legs, sometimes with spade feet, or turned tapering legs. The variety of Hepplewhite's designs was as extensive as Chippendale's: wardrobes (with or without oval door panels of satinwood); chests of drawers; side-boards in several shapes and sizes, bow-fronted, serpentine-fronted, straight, break-fronted; sofas with upholstered sides and backs, or with backs formed by three or even four adjoining chair-backs (sometimes called tri-seat settees or quadri-seat settees); card tables; Pembroke tables with rounded flaps, squared flaps or wavy-edged flaps (incorrectly called butterfly tables), the tables inlaid or banded in satinwood. Hepplewhite may have invented the grandfather chair, an armchair with very high upholstered back and wing sides. His double chests, *commodes*, single chests and clothes presses, had little moulding but were graced with elegant marquetry, or beautifully matched and figured wood panelling. Many of the designs of the marquetry were provided for him by leading artists of the day, such as Angelica Kauffmann, Giovanni-Battista Cipriani (1727–85) (famous for his painted and plastered ceilings), and Antonio Zucchi (1726–95).

Thomas Sheraton (1751–1806) was born at Stockton-on-Tees and became a designer and cabinet-maker. He was also a fervent Baptist and writer on theological problems. As in the case of Hepplewhite, no furniture made by Sheraton has survived, if indeed he ever made any, and his fame was built upon a book of designs. He came to London in about 1790, but does not appear to have set up a workshop. Within a year he had produced the first two parts of a four-part work, *The Cabinet-Maker and Upholsterer's Drawing-book*, in which he described himself as a cabinet-maker, severely criticized the designs in Hepplewhite's book published only a year or so earlier, saying they were out of date, and being equally scathing about Chippendale. The second two parts of the book appeared soon after 1791, and the whole work was reprinted in 1794 and again in 1802, by which later date

Six chair-backs from Sheraton's Drawing Book, *1794*

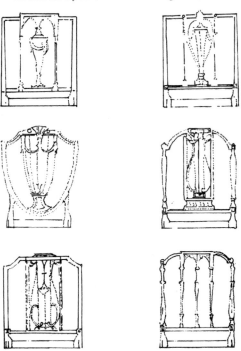

108

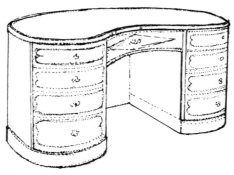

Early 19th cent. English mahogany and satinwood kidney-shaped writing table with drawers, devised by Sheraton and made soon after his death. (1806)

Sheraton had returned to the North to become an ordained Baptist minister. His last six years in Co. Durham were not happy. Despite his reputation as a designer and the interest shown in his works, he fell on hard times and lived in poverty, losing his sanity in about 1805 and dying a year later. Unfinished works containing more of his designs and criticisms appeared in print after his death.

Sheraton's *Drawing-book* had also contained some 300 designs, some of which were repeats of other people's ideas, but many of them his own, and there is no doubt about the high quality and originality of the latter, manifest in the many surviving pieces made according to his designs both during and after his lifetime. Sheraton favoured lighter woods, lighter furniture, painted pieces and pieces with simpler displays of marquetry. The outlines of his furniture are on the whole straighter than Hepplewhite's, notably his chair-backs, and these designs strongly influenced furniture outside Britain as well as at home. His *Drawing-book* contains some intricate pieces, some of them made for women, like small cylinder-top desks, various dressing tables with moving parts for more than one use, work tables and games tables.

The term Regency furniture covers the styles made in Britain from the end of the eighteenth century to the reign of William IV (1830–37), though the Regency itself lasted only from 1811 to 1820. The principal features were more classical Greek and Roman forms, together with other ancient styles such as Egyptian, Persian and even Chinese. Sabre legs for arm- and upright chairs (reminiscent of the Greek *klismos*, see page 33), animal heads with rings for drawer-pulls, animal paws (especially lion paws) for feet on pillar tables and couches, and animal figures for whole legs, or trestles or supports for larger consoles and so forth, were the main characteristics. Woods preferred were darker than those that Hepplewhite and Sheraton chose, and returned to mahogany, Brazilian rosewood and Far Eastern dark woods, brown amboyna, and a striped wood called zebrawood. New techniques included French polishing, machine planing, machine grooving and cutting, and even machine dovetailing. Inlays were built up from coloured woods, ivory, mother-of-pearl, and were also of brass, silver and stone.

Two major exponents of the Regency style were Thomas Hope (1768–1831) a connoisseur and designer, who published *Household Furniture and Interior Decoration* in 1807, and George Smith (active 1804–28), a cabinet-maker, who knew Sheraton and published *A Collection of Designs for Household Furniture and Interior Decoration* in 1808. Hope's two houses, one in Mayfair and another near Dorking, in Surrey, were furnished in classical style to enhance his collection of ancient bronzes, vases, and ceramics. This led him to produce his own book of designs so that others might enjoy the happy decorative environment that he had made for himself. Smith's aim was to take current Regency styles, including the taste for Egyptian motifs arising from Napoleon's campaigns in Egypt at the end of the 1790s, and to interpret them in a popular manner for a growingly wide public able to afford nice pieces of furniture. At the same time, the British did not lose their enthusiasm for things Chinese, and there was also a continued interest in Gothic.

Regency designs persisted into the 1830s and tailed off into the next decade, becoming heavier and coarser, and less inventive. Even before the ascension of Queen Victoria in 1837, machines had

Above, design for early 19th cent. sofa table, from George Smith's Collection of Designs, *1808. Note use of lion motifs for the supports.*

Right, early 19th cent. English Regency 'Trafalgar' upright chair, with rope back and sabre front legs. The name comes from Nelson's great victory at sea, 21 Oct. 1805.

been invented and were being produced which aped the skills of hand-craftsmen and did it in a fraction of the time. It was perhaps inevitable that quality would suffer. There were machines to cut veneers wafer-thin, to carve sculpture out of block wood, to saw planks and to cut frets and trellis out of sheet timber. A flood of cheap furniture in mahogany and other timbers resulted. For decades, furniture was to be produced by machines, with occasional hand-applied embellishment. Few original ideas emerged among the repetitions and mixtures of earlier styles of which the best features were often ignored. Most designs had little merit, though occasionally the quality of materials and of some of the workmanship was commendable. The desire for luxurious display characterized most Victorian decorative art, even in upholstery. The selection of pieces of furniture exhibited at the Great Exhibition in Hyde Park in 1851 showed what manufacturers were capable of making if they really tried, and the quality of exhibits was often high. But to a large extent what was on show was not what was on sale outside, nor what would be on sale in the future, which was generally without grace or refinement. The whole gamut of previous styles was run through, one way or another, and foreign ornamental themes were borrowed and often corrupted. Among popular pieces were bulging upholstered armchairs, sometimes with coiled springs (invented at the end of the 1820s), balloon-back upright chairs, huge square, rectangular, round, oval, polygonal and violin-topped tables on centre pedestals with pronounced feet, or on vast bulb legs, and colossal chests of drawers, wardrobes, sideboards and cabinets, which filled expanses of wall space and towered over the occupants of the rooms.

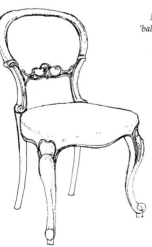

Mid 19th cent. English walnut Victorian 'balloon back' upright chair on cabriole legs, possibly made in time for the Great Exhibition at the Crystal Palace in Hyde Park, 1851.

There had to be a reaction, sooner or later, and it began with the ideas of William Morris (1834–96), poet, author, designer and social reformer, who hated the drab ugliness of industrial towns and their buildings and the pieces with which people furnished them. Craftsmanship seemed to him to have vanished, and it was his dream to resurrect it. This would entail a return to the mediaeval ideal of handicrafts being enjoyable. He set up a business with some friends, working in conjunction with architects like Philip Webb and painters of the pre-Raphaelite school, like Edward Burne-Jones and D.G. Rossetti, to influence all areas of design- architecture, decoration, furnishing, wallpapers, printed textiles, carpets and so forth. His firm sought to recall the work of country carpenters and joiners and chair-makers who were unaffected by modern fashions. Emphasis was put on jointing and construction, to make sound and simple furniture with little or no ornament. Morris's ideas, which he publicized for years in a series of vigorous public lecture programmes, were tremendously influential and led, among other things, to the Art Nouveau movement towards the end of the nineteenth century.

(9) SCANDINAVIA: SIXTEENTH TO NINETEENTH CENTURIES

The Gothic style in furniture had reached Scandinavia in the late Middle Ages, and was modified with interesting local ornament of interlaced designs, with birds, beasts, vines and sporadic inclusion of familiar Viking motifs. Pieces surviving from the fifteenth and sixteenth centuries have a solid, well-put-together look, with carvings on many surfaces. Before the end of the sixteenth century, Renaissance styles had arrived and had begun to displace the Gothic. Danish royal and nobility furniture of the last quarter of the sixteenth century sometimes featured carved coats of arms and Romayne panels with local portraits on chests and cupboards. There was also a liking for linenfold panelling, with variations featuring interwoven flat tracery and flower patterns. Swedish craftsmen made box beds which had cupboards above, beside and below the bed area. Chests were often dome-lidded and exces- sively banded with iron strapwork fixed with closely spaced studding. Some chairs, stools and beds featured the auricular motif in ornamental carving (see page 72). There are also some signs of similarities with English furniture of the Elizabeth period (later sixteenth century), although it is not known which country influenced the other.

In the seventeenth century, Scandinavia began to play a significant rôle in the European scene, particularly Sweden after the decisive contribution by its king, Gustavus Adolphus (1611– 32), who championed the Protestant cause and won many victories over the Catholics in the Thirty Years' War (1618–48). Scandina- vians were drawn in through their close contact with the Hanseatic towns, notably Lübeck, Hamburg and Danzig, all in northern Germany. After the Thirty Years' War the huge ornately carved

Mid 17th cent. Danish oak cupboard door with high quality carved panels.

and panelled cupboards associated with Hamburg and Frankfurt workshops, for example, found favour and were copied in Scandinavia. Then in the last thirty years of the seventeenth century, other influences began to supplement the German, and we find decoration and furniture in French, Dutch and English forms.

English influence stemmed partly from the aftermath of London's Great Fire of 1666, in which nearly 14,000 buildings were destroyed. Huge quantities of timber, more than could be provided from the home market, were needed for rebuilding. England had long been importing timber from the Scandinavians: now the trade intensified, and soon English-made furniture was being exported along with other goods in return for wood. The Scandinavians then began to copy English styles, this time rather slavishly, though sometimes incorporating features of national identity such

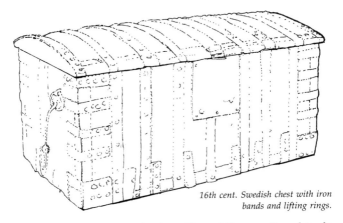

*16th cent. Swedish chest with iron
bands and lifting rings.*

as royal monograms or Viking motifs, and they continued to do
so for a while after the prototypes had ceased to be fashionable in
England. This was particularly the case with Scandinavian chair-
making. Dutch influence was less prevalent, except perhaps in
Denmark which is close to Holland. In the first half of the
eighteenth century, Danish cabinet-makers were making break-
fronted chests, and their marquetry, particularly of flowers, often
showed the influence of Holland.

The English and Dutch styles, however popular, were enjoyed
mostly by the Scandinavian middle classes. Royal families and
nobles on the whole preferred French styles, and this comple-
mented their growing enthusiasm for French palatial architecture.

Early 17th cent. Danish oak side table with shallow drawer in centre.

Left, 18th cent. Swedish Rococo style bombé commode by Gustav Foltiern (c.1770).

Below left, 18th cent. Danish beechwood upright chair in the manner of Chippendale, 1767–8

Below, 18th cent. Norwegian walnut armchair in Chippendale manner, c.1770

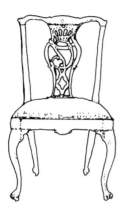

At the outset of the eighteenth century, new mansions were being built in the French manner and decorated and furnished likewise. These ideas eventually percolated downwards to the middle classes, especially in Sweden, where many native craftsmen visited Paris to study French methods and then came home to put them into practice. In all three countries, French styles were of course modified by national idiosyncracies, and quite often pieces like chairs were constructed using local traditional woods like the traditional oak, birch and pine.

The Rococo style was popular in both Sweden and Denmark in the mid-eighteenth century, but some (though not all) of the pieces do look as if they were influenced more by German over-elaboration of the curves than by pure French Rococo. A *commode* by Foltiern of Stockholm, of about 1770, for example, would never have been made in Paris. Yet within a few years, the Swedish cabinet-maker Georg Haupt (1741–84), who had studied in Paris, produced excellent examples of Louis XVI furniture, including a *bureau plat* for the Swedish king, Gustav III, who was pro-French. At the same time, English influences persisted in Scandinavia. Two chairs in the Chippendale manner illustrate this, one, a Danish beechwood upright of about 1768 and a Norwegian walnut armchair of about 1770 (top, page 115). Their design is said to have been taken directly from Chippendale's *Director* (see page 102). In the 1790s, many Danish craftsmen worked in London where they studied the pattern books of George Hepplewhite, Thomas Sheraton (see page 108) and others. Mahogany was introduced to Danish craftsmen on a wide scale, and its use spread to Sweden.

Danish Louis XVI style furniture developed along German rather than French lines, with cupboards consisting of two or three stages and chairs having both German and English features. The enthusiasm for these neo-classical styles in Sweden was advanced by the work of Louis Masreliez, a leading designer who had worked in Rome for several years, and who brought ideas back to Swedish craftsmen in drawings as well as in pieces that he made or commissioned.

During the first two decades of the nineteenth century, the taste for English styles received a blow, partly because of anger at Nelson's destruction of the Danish fleet in harbour at Copenhagen and partly as a result of Napoleon's mastery of Europe, which affected trade with Britain. This cut down the amount of English furniture reaching Scandinavia. Instead, tastes turned towards the French Empire style, since French and German furniture was easily imported and, presumably, Scandinavian craftsmen could travel without interference to France, Germany and Italy, to study styles and methods. Out of this developed a Danish Empire style, based on French Empire but marked by its own simplicity, with a leaning towards stricter classical themes. This style prevailed in Denmark right into the mid-nineteenth century. As mahogany, from which

Sketches of chairs in classical style by the Swedish designer Louis Masreliez, in the 1780s.

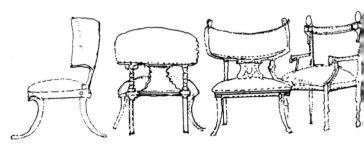

French Empire furniture had for a time principally been made, was not always easy to obtain, the Danes used their native maple, birch and ash. Birch is much like satinwood at first sight, and was a very good substitute for veneering, stringing, and solid work. Mounts were either of metal (usually brass) or were carved in wood and gilded to look like brass or bronze. In Sweden, Empire furniture was on the whole more faithful to French Empire, but the growing trend towards mechanizing woodworking skills led to a fall in the high standards of cabinet-making.

Early 19th cent. Danish 3-stage oak cupboard (or escritoire) with veneer of mahogany and other woods, and with gilt bronze mounts.

Late 18th cent. Swedish mahogany fall-front bureau by Iwersson of Stockholm, in the English manner, c.1790.

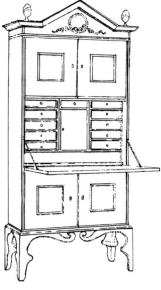

(10) RUSSIA AND POLAND: SEVENTEENTH TO NINETEENTH CENTURIES

In this work, discussion of East European furniture of the seventeenth to nineteenth centuries is confined to developments in Russia and Poland. Until the time of Peter the Great, Czar of Russia from 1682 to 1725, Russia was only occasionally affected by the architectural and decorative movements of Western Europe. Although the history of Russia's own unique architecture and building styles, and the astonishingly varied things Russians could and did do with timber, reach back into the Middle Ages and are a fascinating subject on their own, Russian furniture did not begin to display a similar creativity until the later seventeenth century. Before Peter the Great, Russian craftsmen had already begun to make interesting and useful household furniture and, with centuries of woodworking skill behind them, were splendidly equipped to take advantage of the Czar's introduction of Western ideas to his realm. In his efforts to 'westernize' Russia, he was ruthless in curbing indigenous artistic traditions, but we shall see that these could not be suppressed.

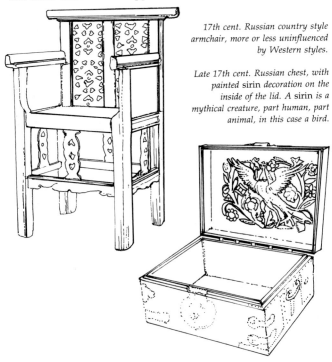

17th cent. Russian country style armchair, more or less uninfluenced by Western styles.

Late 17th cent. Russian chest, with painted sirin decoration on the inside of the lid. A sirin is a mythical creature, part human, part animal, in this case a bird.

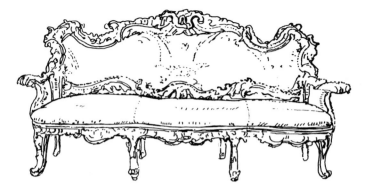

Splendidly ornate mid 18th cent. Russian settee from a design by Bartolommeo Rastrelli in bold Rococo style, c.1740–50.

As a young man, Peter the Great had travelled extensively in Western Europe, and even worked in disguise as a carpenter in Holland and at Deptford in England. When he returned, he ordered large quantities of furniture from the Low Countries, Britain and France to be brought to Russia for craftsmen to examine and copy. He founded a new capital city in the north, St Petersburg, which had to be built from scratch and chiefly in stone, instead of in traditional timber. He compelled the nobility to contribute towards the great project by making them build new homes for themselves in the city, whether they required new homes or not. And they had to furnish them with Western style furniture. To assist in the decoration of his own new buildings, Peter the Great employed Carlo Rastrelli (d.1744), the Florentine sculptor and designer.

The earliest of the new Russian furniture was in the Baroque style, and this was followed by Rococo and that in turn by neo-classical. Russian pieces were often larger than their counterparts in the West, even if only by an inch or so all round, and the decoration was sometimes heavier, occasionally coarser, but withal very well made. The Rococo style became widely fashionable in the eighteenth century, under the stimulus of Rastrelli's son, Bartolommeo (1700–71). He designed and decorated the Palace of Tsarskoe Selo and the Winter Palace for Peter the Great's daughter, Czarina Elizabeth II (1741–62) (who once had a house built for her entirely in timber, erected within twenty-four hours). Rastrelli's work, most particularly his seat furniture, such as large sofas and chairs, is unmistakably Russian – sumptuous and never dull.

When German-born Catherine (the Great) became Czarina in 1762, after having disposed of her husband, Czar Paul, she employed French *ébénistes* to work in St Petersburg and elsewhere, and also commissioned numerous pieces from the Paris workshops. She encouraged craftsmen from her native Germany as well, and ordered over one hundred items from the Roentgens' workshop at Neuwied alone.

If royalty and the nobility indulged themselves in costly furnishings according to prevailing French and German styles, ordinary people were not deprived of good furniture in more strictly national styles. In the eighteenth century, there was a new and quite unusual range of pieces made of polished steel by workshops in the city of Tula, about one hundred miles south of Moscow. Tula had had a large government ordnance factory installed there in about 1710 by Peter the Great. This unusually attractive and functional furniture included chairs, tables, stools and dressing tables, in which the principal characteristic was open fretwork or tracery in backs, sides, seats and even structural members. It was essentially Russian, although Western motifs were occasionally incorporated. This may in part be due to the fact that Catherine once visited the English Midlands, where at Matthew Boulton's factory complex in Birmingham, she saw cut and polished steel artefacts, including experimental furniture. Certainly, she encouraged the Tula industry by ordering pieces for imperial buildings, and Tula furniture was to become fashionable right across Russia. There is a Tula armchair in the Victoria & Albert Museum but the one illustrated is at present in The Hermitage in St Petersburg.

Late eighteenth century neo-classical styles began to supplant the Rococo in Russia in the last quarter of the eighteenth century, but it is interesting to see from the Hermitage catalogues, and those of Tsarskoe Selo and elsewhere, that the Russian native elements are strongly present in much furniture made from about 1775 to around the 1830s. These elements include profuse – and occasionally excessive – ornament, applied sometimes to simpler forms and not always as well executed as in the West.

Mid 18th cent. Russian Tula steel armchair with seat cushion, mounted on large casters. Now in the State Hermitage Museum, St Petersburg.

Much seat furniture was still on the substantial side: arms, seat rails and crests, all seem larger than their counterparts in, say, Britain, particularly in chairs roughly derivative of Sheraton designs. Thus, when the Directoire and Empire styles reached Russia in the first years of the nineteenth century, it is no surprise to find that pieces were even heavier-looking than the French. Yet there was compensation in the consistently high standards of construction that Russian furniture-makers maintained.

For almost the entire first half of the nineteenth century, Russian furniture followed the dominant European fashion. There were Russian Biedermeier, Russian versions of Louis Philippe, versions of eighteenth-century French and Russian Sheraton. Pieces were made in mahogany, but more were made in native woods, such as birch and oak. An armchair of birch and other woods of the 1820s reveals the influence of English Regency mixed with French Empire.

Late 18th cent. Russian double cupboard with intarsia work pictures of classical scenes set in an otherwise simple framework.

Late 18th cent. Russian armchair of unusual design, particularly the arms and cresting made in one sweep.

In the 1850s and 1860s, there was a definite move away from reproductions of Western forms, to create a more national corpus of pieces, in which the ecclesiastical element returned, with chairs having arch backs, and cupboards and chests severely rectilinear and with very simple ornament.

Western European styles were also influential in the furniture of Poland, particularly in the middle and later eighteenth century. Up to about the 1740s, much furniture, especially provincial, was heavy and over-bearing rather like the North German pieces, (sometimes it is hard to distinguish Danzig cupboards from native Polish cupboards of the same period). Much furniture was decorated with primitive inlays (marquetry might be too complimentary a word for some of it). Decoration incorporated natural subjects like flowers and birds. In Warsaw and Cracow, eighteenth-century French influences affected furniture made for royalty and nobility. The Poles were fascinated by the Rococo, and great houses in the style were designed by French architects and artists like Juste-Aurèle Meissonnier (1695–1750) and Nicholas Pineau (1684–1754). French and German *ébénistes* were invited to Poland to direct furniture-making in local workshops. Others in Paris made pieces to order, especially for King Stanislaus Poniatowski, (1764–95). But in spite of the directness of French influence, Polish Rococo in general appears less gay and lively. Some pieces even look quite sombre.

Mid 18th cent. Polish cupboard on stand, decorated in marquetry of elm, oak and green-dyed walnut.

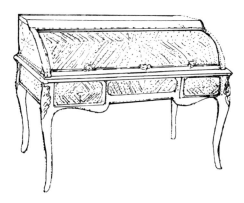

Late 18th cent. Polish cylinder-top desk made in Warsaw in French style (c.1775)

In the last years of the century, Poland suffered cruelly at the hands of its larger neighbours, Austria, Prussia and Russia, who partitioned the ancient land three times between 1772 and 1795. The social and economic distress which followed did not help native Polish craftsmanship to flourish, yet many pieces of the time are nevertheless fine. This was because, despite the disruptions and the contraction of the kingdom during his reign, Stanislaus invited numerous German craftsmen to work in Warsaw, where they made quantities of furniture for him and his nobles. Some of the workshops established by these German craftsmen were still producing furniture well into the nineteenth century.

After the defeat of Napoleon in 1815, the unity and independence that Poland had hoped for in the latter's creation of the Grand Duchy of Warsaw, receded and the country remained partitioned for another century. But if Poles were not free to make their own affairs, Polish culture was not extinguished. In Polish furniture workshops, whether established by Stanislaus's German emigrants in the previous century or run by native craftsmen, a considerable amount of furniture was produced over many decades, characterized by strong regional interpretations of European movements. Poland was still to some extent feudal, in that local lords ruled over tenants and peasants in a land that was still largely agricultural. Historians refer to workshops on baronial estates where craftsmen continued to make traditional furniture, decade after decade, while in towns like Warsaw and Cracow, more international styles were copied and adapted, among them Biedermeier, neo-Gothic, and English post-Regency and early Victorian.

AMERICAS

(1) PRE-COLUMBIAN TO SIXTEENTH CENTURY

The pre-Columbian civilizations of America stretched back over thirty centuries before the arrival of Columbus at one of the Bahama Islands in October 1492. The most recent – and the best-known because it was they who fell to the Spanish conquistadores in the early sixteenth century – were the Aztecs in Mexico and the Incas in Peru. Their predecessors were a fascinating variety of civilizations and cultures, such as the Olmecs, the Maya and the Toltecs in the north, and the Chavin de Huantar, the Nazca, the Mochica and the Chimu in the south. Sadly, the Spaniards robbed the Americas of almost all the treasure in precious metals and stones they could lay their hands on, and also wilfully destroyed more or less everything else that would succumb to fire or pulverizing. Huge quantities of Inca furniture and other household effects, for example, were burned; contemporary Spanish writers noted a particularly large bonfire at the Inca capital, Cuzco, in Peru.

Although numerous relics have been found as a result of excavations, great gaps remain in our knowledge of everyday life in pre-Columbian America. One such gap concerns the furniture, of which little of any kind has survived, either in solid form or in contemporary illustration. And while in the many histories of pre-Columbian America there are numerous descriptions of palaces, temples and houses, great and small, relating to every one of the civilizations, identification of the furniture inside these buildings is extremely rare.

Among the earliest details we have is the fact that beds used by the people of the late Classic period of the Maya (ADc.600–c.1000) in central America were made of racks of tough, flexible, thin branches of trees stretched across wooden frames. Kitchens, in simpler homes, had some kind of table and a few stools, though

A Toltec jaguar throne or seat of stone, from Chichen Itza, c.12–14 century. It was painted red and inlaid with jade, and used by a Toltec noble.

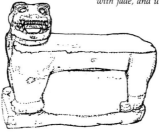

A 14th cent. Central American stone table with dished top, used for offerings to gods, from the Chiriqui culture in Panama.

the shapes are not exactly known. A seat of a noble at Chichen Itza, a Maya site later developed by the Toltecs in the eleventh century, was made of stone in the shape of a jaguar whose back was rendered flat between the head and the tail. The 'chair' legs were the front and rear paws of the jaguar. The jaguar was a symbol of a late Maya order of nobility, and one that had considerable religious significance in other pre-Columbian cultures.

In the Mochica civilization in South America (AD c.300–c.1000), some chiefs are portrayed in paintings sitting on stepped thrones. In the fourteenth century, the Central Americans of Chiriqui (now Panama) made stone tables with sculptured human-figure supports. Some of the table tops were *dished* for offerings to the gods.

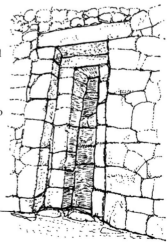

A wall niche in an Inca building of the 15th cent, in Cuzco, Peru, South America. The niche may have had removable shelves.

A Chimu civilization carved wooden work box from Peru, S. America. 14th cent.

In the time of the Incas in South America (*c*.1300–*c*.1530) top people often sat on low benches which were usually decorated; if the bench was for the Inca emperor himself, it would be veneered and ornamented in gold. Stone building remains in Peru show that in some rooms, niches were inset in walls to allow ranges of shelves for displaying ornaments and/or storing drinking vessels, cooking pots, other utensils and so forth. These shelves would have been of wood or stone. Remains of household items made of wood have survived, some in a nearly complete state. The fourteenth-century carved work-box above belonged to a Chimu civilization house-wife, living in the capital, ChanChan, on the north-west coast of Peru.

(2) UNITED STATES: SEVENTEENTH TO NINETEENTH CENTURIES

The furniture of the American Colonies was handsome, vigorous and in many respects original. The first colonists embarking in small ships from Britain could not take the complete contents of all their homes with them to the New World. They had therefore to make new furniture once they settled. For those who were craftsmen this would not of course have been a problem. The earliest pieces resembled the British styles the settlers had grown up with, especially those which were characterized by Puritan simplicity, but the furniture they made in America also had strongly individual characteristics. What is more, they were well made, and surviving authentic examples are to day highly valued in the USA.

Apart from the simplicity, there are other distinctive characteristics. One was that in many categories of furniture, pieces were often a little narrower and a little taller than the styles in Britain. Another was that the colonists found ready to hand some hitherto unfamiliar woods for furniture-making, woods such as maple, poplar and hickory, and they worked these, along with more traditional oak, pine, ash and elm, with great skill. The freedom they enjoyed in a new land seemed to liberate the inventiveness of the craftsmen and this resulted in new styles and more varied experiment with existing styles. American Jacobean furniture, for example, was well-proportioned and the range extensive. Press or court cupboards were like Flemish models or the Welsh *cwpwrdd deuddarn* and *cwprwdd tridarn*, but often had carved strapwork and split baluster moulding. Chests of drawers displayed inventiveness. Many were painted in several colours. Some had five rows of drawers instead of the conventional three or four, and the number of drawers in line varied as well. Chests with drawers underneath – incorrectly called mule chests – received some fine decorative treatment, with relief floral carving and split baluster applied moulding on the front, or flat carving of flowers and/or foliage. Some good examples have survived.

American chairs of the seventeenth century were often idiosyncratic variants of contemporary British types, particularly the joined armchair with panel back, which sometimes had architectural supports. Colonists also made versions of the traditional English 'thrown' chair (see colour section). From this came two particular types, often called the Brewster and the Carver chairs. One type had spindles below the seat rail in front and between the arms and the side rails, the other had no spindles. The former (Brewster) chair has been said to have been designed by William Brewster, one of the original Pilgrim Fathers in the Mayflower, the latter (Carver) by John Carver, another Mayflower passenger. There is no evidence for this, even if one or other did actually possess one or more chairs subsequently named after him. What

A late 17th cent. colonial American oak joined chest of five rows of drawers, painted in white, red and black, of c.1678, made in Ipswich, Mass.

are more reliable and distinct colonist features of the 'thrown' chair are the facts that in the northern colonies the arm of the armchair was usually mortised into the back and into the front stiles, the latter being capped by a turned mushroom type disc or a ball, while the armchair of the more southerly colonies had the front join made by the style top fitting into a slot in the arm.

Eighteenth century American furniture had the best of all worlds – freedom of expression, a marvellous range of available woods, craftsmen of the highest skills, not only British or of British descent but also of continental origin. These craftsmen had the pick of all European styles to copy and develop, and the motivation to innovate as well. That for most of the century they chose to adopt and adapt British styles more frequently than others may well lie in the innate conservatism of the British craftsmen which predominated in America, and which we have noted earlier (page 93). Another reason may lie in the wide availability of English pattern books of design and ornament, which are known to have been imported as soon as they were published in England. Chippendale's *Director* was neither the first nor the last, but it was probably the most influential (see below, page 130) of these. Whatever the reasons, there is no questioining the very high achievement of American cabinet-making and woodwork.

William and Mary styles (see page 100) became fashionable in America at the close of the seventeenth century, and popular pieces now included chests-on-chests, chests-on-stands and side tables. The last two items came to be known, respectively, in America as highboys and lowboys. The type of side table given the name lowboy was one which had a wide drawer immediately under the top and right across the piece, and a narrow and often deeper drawers below. The space between them was sometimes filled by a shaped and carved decorative panel. Occasionally, there might be a pair of drawers side-by-side in the topline instead of a single drawer. This type of side table was the same or very similar to the lower section of a chest-on-stand. Another kind of table was the gate-legged variety, popular in Britain since the late sixteenth century, and a 'relative', the butterfly drop-leaf table, so named not from any shaping of the leaves but of the wing brackets under the table top which opened out to support the leaves. One distinctive feature of these American tables was that the four legs splayed outwards at 5 to 10 degrees off the vertical for extra stability and were linked by low turned stretchers. At this time, there were also cabinet pieces called secretaries (as distinct from *secrétaires*) and these were the American equivalent of the bureau-bookcase or slope-fronted desk, with drawers under and surmounted by a bookcase cupboard with panelled or glazed doors. There were also fine upholstered armchairs with rolled wing arms, nearly always on cabriole legs.

The Queen Anne style (see page 101) reached America in the second decade, and is best illustrated by the wide use of the

Above, early 18th cent. colonial American maplewood 'butterfly' table, made in New England.

Left, mid 18th cent. colonial Queen Anne style walnut upright chair, with stretchers and claw and ball feet.

cabriole leg for chairs, for the stands of highboys, for some tables and for other seat furniture. The main features of American Queen Anne were more curvilinear forms of William and Mary styles, and in this period some very fine chairs were made in walnut, lacquered wood, mahogany, hickory, maple and oak, in which the claw and ball foot at the end of the leg was prominent. Highboys were more gracefully shaped and more profusely carved and decorated, and we see the emergence of the famous recessed shell and the 'sunburst' ornament, often carved in birchwood, in the apron of the stand between the two lowest drawers. The 'sunburst' looked like a sun's rays. The motif was sometimes repeated on the top section of the piece, between the topmost two drawers and the pediment or cornice. [See cover illustration.]

Chairs were often exquisitely made, with shaped solid or pierced splats, curvilinear crests, and shells carved on the knees of vigorous and robust cabriole legs. Some of these chairs had turned stretchers between front and back legs and a connecting stretcher between. The style continued until the middle of the century and was followed by American Chippendale. The early Georgian style in Britain was almost completely by-passed.

American Chippendale appeared in the 1750s. Although Chippendale book designs did not appear in print until 1754 (with a reprint the next year), there is evidence that some of the designs had reached America in advance, and this has resulted in a quantity of American Chippendale pieces that can be confidently dated in the 1750s. Among the principal features were the continuing use of cabriole legs for chairs, tables and stands, and concurrently more use of the straight, square leg with variants such as the canted inner edge, or convex-moulded surfaces to the outer sides (sometimes referred to as 'toad-back' moulding). The cabriole leg still terminated in a claw and ball foot, but other types employed included the volute foot, the hoof foot and the claw foot without the ball.

Although the range of American Chippendale furniture was considerable, much emphasis was put on chests-on-chests (also known as double chests) and chests-on-stands (highboys). The American Chippendale style which lasted for thirty or more years, also saw the American innovation of the block front on chests, *bureaux*, desks, highboys and kneehole tables. This is a feature where a drawer front, or a vertical row of drawer fronts, is cut to produce a raised surface at each end and a recessed surface in between, and it was usually produced from a single piece of wood, though glueing an outer strip of wood on each end was not unknown. This feature was prominent in New England, devised and popularized by two cabinet-makers in Newport, Rhode island,

Mid 18th cent. colonial American Chippendale shell-carved and block front mahogany kneehole dressing table by Goddard & Townend family, Rhode Island, 1765.

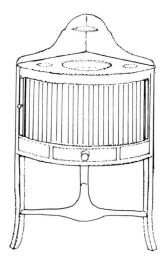

Late 18th cent. U.S. mahogany and satinwood tambour-front wash stand, probably by John Seymour of Boston, 1790–1800.

John Goddard (1723–85) and John Townsend (1721–1809), who pioneered a great deal of American Chippendale styles. The principal district for the best of Chippendale, however, was Philadelphia where much Rococo furniture was made, including some very fine mirrors and some interesting decorated chests of drawers. Among the main craftsmen were Benjamin Randolph (1721–91), Thomas Affleck (1740–95), a Scottish emigrant who set up in business in 1760, and William Savery (1721–88).

The growing bitterness between the colonists and the home government in Britain in the 1760s and 1770s, culminating in their successful war of independence and the break-away in 1783, cut back, if it did not absolutely close down on, commercial relations. This prevented the newly arrived and very popular Adam style in Britain reaching America, beyond the odd design in one or two workshops, and American Chippendale continued to flourish right to about 1790. Then, the mainstream of new furniture styling was to be Hepplewhite and Sheraton rather than Adam. This period in American furniture is generally called the Federal Style, and it went on to about 1830, and included something of the unattractive Directoire and Empire styles of France.

The Federal style began when the drawings by Hepplewhite and Sheraton arrived in America, and were enthusiastically taken up by many leading craftsmen. Among these were Scottish emigrant cabinet-makers like Duncan Phyfe (1768–1854), a Sheraton devotee and also attracted to Hepplewhite, and Samuel McIntire (1757–1811) who also favoured both. Hepplewhite style was popular to about 1800; Sheraton lasted somewhat longer. Carving, inlay, marquetry, all were the vogue decorative treatments, with flowers, foliage, swags in front, and the preferred wood was mahogany, with satinwood as accessory. Pieces wanted included *commodes*, card-tables (often in pairs so that they could be used when folded as side tables against the wall), sideboards, secretaries, desks and a variety of chairs, bar-backed, rope-backed, lyre-backed, shield-backed (a Hepplewhite speciality), and cane seated or upholstered and overstuffed. Much use of satinwood was made for inlays of ovals, strings, shells, paterae and so forth.

Alongside these British modes ran the American Directoire (c.1805–1815) inspired by French Directoire, in which Duncan Phyfe made many pieces including hexagonal card-tables, Grecian chairs, and Roman couch-shaped sofas. Towards the end of the short Directoire periods American Empire (c.1810–1840) with its stronger French base but yet having Sheratonian imprints, emerged. Some of it was 'coarse, massive and cumbrous' as one celebrated American furniture historian (Louise Ada Boger) put it, whose main features were rounded columns on carcase furniture, huge lion's paw feet, and a plethora of carved eagles, horns, chimerae, sphinxes, exaggerated and shaggy paw feet of other animals, real and imaginary, applied to chairs, three- or four-foot

Early 19th cent. U.S. Federal style mahogany swivel top card-table by Duncan Phyfe, c.1805.

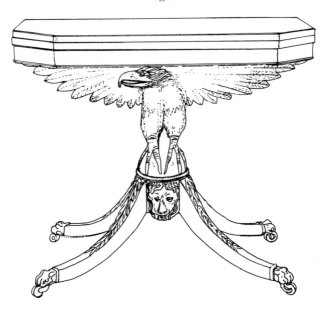

Mid 19th cent. U.S. rosewood and mahogany upright chair, in a mix of styles, notably the 17th cent. legs and stiles, and early 18th cent. carved back, with overstuffed seat of more unusual 19th cent. style.

pedestal bases, consoles and so forth. Duncan Phyfe was again prominent in this style, though several American furniture historians regard his last works as inferior to what went before.

After the 1830s, and for several decades, American furniture seemed to go through various earlier styles all over again, but with nineteenth-century modifications, assisted with mechanical processes such as veneer-cutting machines, mass-production of applied decorative features, mechanical planes, saws, and so on. Very often the styles were mixed, and it was not impossible to see a chair of basic late sixteenth-century form, with seventeenth-century swash turned uprights, Baroque cresting rail, even Rococo scroll back or Queen Anne type splat, on cabriole or turned legs. Then in the mid-nineteenth century we see the arrival in America of the renewed rage for Gothic revival from Britain and the continent, though it did not affect furniture to anything like the extent it had in Europe. Nor did it last long. The style is architectural rather than decorative. After the Civil War (1861–65) and the tremendous upheaval it brought about in American society, there was a return to some of the eighteenth-century French styles, notably Rococo and Louis XVI, but these revivals were neither faithful nor fine reproductions. They were as a rule heavier and disproportionate, though there were some remarkably well-crafted copies, particularly from the New York firm headed by J.H. Belter who used laminated wood and achieved fine effects, and George Henkels of Philadelphia.

A word should be said about a totally different and quite original style of furniture made by a religious sect, the Shakers, which originated in Britain and emigrated to America in the 1770s to settle in New England. They were extreme Puritans, believing in, if not always practising, celibacy. Their simplicity was reflected in the furniture they made for their own community which lived in secluded environments away from other people. The furniture was well proportioned and properly made, with absolutely no decoration. Although functional, it has, probably despite its makers' intentions, a certain elegance, sometimes even beauty. The Shakers made all they needed – chairs, tables, chests of drawers, benches and desks, and the woods they used were locally obtainable, namely pine, fruit, walnut and birch.

A good example of Shaker simplicity in furniture design. This pine and fruitwood small table of the 2nd quarter of the 19th century was made at a Shaker community workshop.

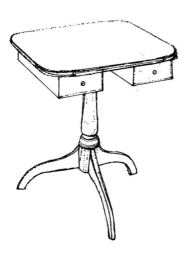

Appendix

(1) ART NOUVEAU FURNITURE

The Art Nouveau movement can be seen partly as a solution to the problem which William Morris and his associates were unable to resolve (see page 112). They believed that art should be 'by the people for the people', and advocated a revival of the crafts and a return to hand-craftsmanship, because machine-made goods were manifestly not as well made, since a workforce operating mass-production machinery, turning out 'shoddy' artefacts, could not obtain the same sort of job satisfaction. That was all very well, but hand-made goods cost much more to make and much more to buy, so taking them out of the reach of all but the wealthy and leisured classes, and also reducing the number of people making a living out of quality workmanship. The dilemma was addressed in the 1870s not so much in England as in France where Morris's ideas had struck a very sympathetic chord.

An organization called Union Centrale des Arts Décoratifs was formed in 1877 in Paris, which aimed to bring together the artist and the designer with the manufacturer, so that the former might be able to design for industrial production and 'thereby serve the common man and not only the connoisseur'. The activities of the Union were co-ordinated with similar aims being institutionalized in other countries, such as Britain, Belgium and the U.S.A. A number of artist-designers and architects became prominent in this movement, notably Morris himself, Arthur Mackurdo and Charles Rennie Mackintosh (Britain), Henri van de Velde and Victor Horta (Belgium), Louis Tiffany (USA) and Eugène Grasset, Emile Galle (glass designer) and Louis Majorelle (France), to mention a few. All contributed to a corpus of new styles of ornament and design in architecture (such as Mackintosh), furniture (van de Velde) and glass (Galle). This resulted in a new fashion whose principal motifs were taken from natural sources such as waves, plants, flowers and flowing hair, applied in 'sinuous curves and convolutions'. The movement was called the Art Nouveau movement, after La

Fine example of Art Nouveau furniture, this oak desk was designed and made by Henri van de Velde in 1896, in Belgium.

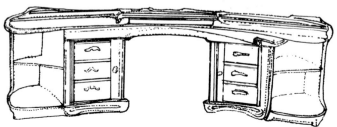

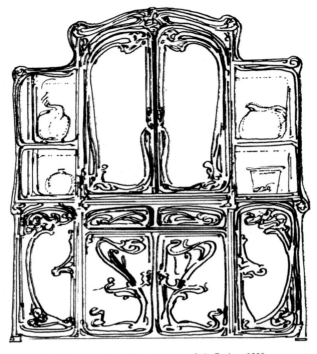

Art Nouveau cabinet of two stages, made in Paris, c.1900.

Maison de l'Art Nouveau, a Paris shop which in 1894/5 began to sell artefacts, furniture, glass and so forth in the new style.

Applied to furniture, Art Nouveau contained features like stained glass flowers and panels in cabinet backs, sides and front doors, painted leaves and flowers in wavy-shaped cartouches or spandrels on flat surfaces, elongated stiles, muntins and rails in chairs, sinuous plant stems as moulding on doors, drawer fronts and table legs. Even the outlines of desk, cabinet and cupboard furniture were a mass of asymmetrical flowing quite unlike anything seen on furniture before. New patterns spread to everything in furniture, to handles, lockplates, hinges, escutcheons, and so forth. Nearly every European country produced its own Art Nouveau, following the prevailing motifs and inventing their own fantasies. Inasmuch as it is possible to date these periods at all, the Art Nouveau movement spanned the years *c.*1890 to *c.*1910. but in that time a huge quantity of furniture in Art Nouveau styles was produced.

(2) STAMPING OF PIECES OF EIGHTEENTH-CENTURY PARIS FURNITURE

The practice of stamping pieces of furniture by the makers was a requirement of membership of the *Corporation des Menuisiers-Ébénistes*, the guild for furniture-makers in Paris. These obligations were re-defined and strengthened in the years 1744 to 1751 by a new set of regulations for the guild. To succeed in the craft, either as *menuisier* or *ébéniste* (before 1744, the difference between the two, though accepted in practice, was not formally recognized by the guild), a furniture-maker had to belong to the guild. This protected members from outside competition and made it easy for them to involve their families by encouraging them to apprentice their sons into the craft. Several top *ébénistes* of earlier years, such as F. Delorme, Pierre Roussel and Pierre Migeon, had sons working under them, who in later years produced fine pieces themselves.

Craftsmen aimed to get their certificate to become a *maître*. This entailed several years' apprenticeship, including a requirement to make at least one piece of high quality which would have to pass scrutiny by a panel of *maîtres*. As soon as a craftsman became a *maître* he could hire assistants with a view to their becoming *maîtres* in due course. This is how the guild enlarged itself. Sometimes a *maître* died and his business was taken on by his widow. There were occasions when the widow married the senior assistant who became chief of the workshop. The most famous example of this was Jean-François Oeben's widow who married Jean-Henri Riesener in 1768.

Among the 1744–51 regulations was one that compelled *maîtres* to stamp their names on the furniture they made. He had to own

The maker's stamp of Georges Jacob, one of the foremost menuisiers of the later 18th cent. in Paris, as struck on the inside of a seat rail of one of his upright chairs.

a special tool, called a *maindron*, an iron stamp bearing his name in relief, which was to be struck with a hammer on every piece leaving his workshop to be sold. The *maindron* was struck on the back, or underneath the carcase, or on the top under the marble slab (if there was one). The mark itself was registered on a lead plate kept by the guild at headquarters. If the piece was acceptable to the guild when completed, then the initials J.M.E., that is, *Jurande Des Menuisiers-Ébénistes*, were stamped near the maker's stamp. Of course, many pieces escaped scrutiny.

A kind of mythology has grown up around these stamps. Pieces sold today that bear a stamp are often, though generally wrongly, considered better, or more valuable, than those without a stamp. Pieces made directly for the Crown were exempt from this rule, however, and since most of the finest furniture of the time was being made for the Crown, the best pieces would most probably be un-stamped. Despite the rule, pieces were stamped in the eighteenth century for a variety of reasons apart from the fact that they were made by such and such a maker. Stamps were used by sons of *maîtres* before they attempted to become *maîtres* themselves. Stamps also had to be used by a *maître* even if all he did was repair a piece made by someone else. Some stamps were used by the workshop *maître* even if he had sold the pieces but had not made them. Léonard Boudin (*maître*, 1761), for example, was known as a dealer as well as a master craftsman. And, of course, makers' *maindrons* have been forged, then and ever since. Nor is it unknown to find one piece bearing two quite different stamps on it.

(3) FURNITURE COLLECTIONS AROUND THE WORLD

The principal public collections of antique furniture contain many examples of pieces from various countries. These collections are generally located in major museums, universities, other institutions and in some privately owned homes that are occasionally open to the public. Many collections specialize in the furniture of one or two particular countries, others have collections centred on periods of furniture, embracing a variety of national styles. Some of these collections are subject to re-arrangement and changes of emphasis from time to time. The list of collections below is arranged under individual countries or, where it is more appropriate, under more general headings. It is not a complete list, but it covers the main periods of furniture from all parts of the world that are mentioned in this book.

AFRICA

Metropolitan Museum of Art, New York, USA; Royal Ontario Museum, Toronto, Canada; Indianapolis Museum of Art, Indiana, USA; Atkins Museum, Kansas City, Missouri, USA; Fine Arts Museum of San Francisco, USA; Brooks Memorial Art Gallery, Memphis, USA; Brooklyn Museum, New York, USA;

Milwaukee Public Museum, Wisconsin, USA; Museum of
Cultural History, University of California, USA; University of
Ghana, Accra, Ghana, West Africa; University of Ife, Nigeria,
West Africa; Museum of African Art, Washington, USA; Indiana
University Art Museum, Bloomington, USA; Museum of African
Art, Washington, DC., USA; American Museum of Natural
History, New York, USA; Musée Royal de L'Afrique Centrale,
Belgium; William Moore Collection, Los Angeles, USA; St Louis
Art Museum, St Louis, Missouri, USA; Katherine White
Collection, Seattle, Washington, USA; University Museum,
University of Pennsylvania, Philadelphia, USA; Peabody
Museum, Harvard, Cambridge, Mass., USA

ANCIENT EGYPT

National Museum, Cairo; Museo Archeologico, Turin, Italy;
Louvre, Paris; British Museum, London; Ashmolean Museum,
Oxford; Museum of Archaeology and Anthropology, Cambridge;
Egyptian Museum, Berlin; Egyptiska Museet, Stockholm, Sweden

ANCIENT GREECE

Rijksmuseum van Oudheden, Leiden, Holland; Dipylon Burial
Place, Athens, Greece; National Museum, Athens, Greece;
Louvre, Paris; British Museum, London; Museo Nazionale,
Naples, Italy

ANCIENT NEAR EAST

Tehran Museum, Iran; Oriental History Institute, Chicago, USA;
Metropolitan Museum of Art, New York, USA; Victoria & Albert
Museum, London; British Museum, London; Louvre, Paris

BRITISH ISLES (selected)

Castle Museum, York; Fairfax House, York; Museum of English
Rural Life, Reading; Haddon Hall, Derbyshire; Victoria & Albert
Museum, London; Lady Lever Art Gallery, Port Sunlight,
Cheshire; Glasgow School of Art, Glasgow, Scotland; Burrell
Collection, Glasgow, Scotland; City Museum, Carlisle, Cumbria;
Lyme Hall, Stockport, Cheshire; Christchurch Mansion, Ipswich,
Suffolk; Saltram House, Plymouth, Devon; Museum of Welsh
Antiquities, Bangor, N. Wales; Bowes Museum, Co. Durham;
Wythenshawe Hall, Manchester; Wallace Collection, Manchester
Square, London; Geffrye Museum, Shoreditch, London;
Courtauld Institute of Art, London; Wilberforce Museum, Hull,
Humberside; Towneley Hall Museum, Burnley, Lancashire; Art
Gallery and Museum, Brighton, Sussex; Aston Hall,
Birmingham; Cecil Higgins Museum, Bedford; William Morris
Gallery, Walthamstow, London; Audley End, Saffron Walden,
Essex; Ham House, Richmond, Surrey; Sir John Soane's
Museum, Lincoln's Inn Fields, London; Chatsworth House,
Bakewell, Derbyshire; Royal Pavilion, Brighton, Sussex; Knole

House, Sevenoaks, Kent; Harewood House, Nr Leeds, Yorkshire; Osterley Park, Middlesex; National Museum of Wales, Cardiff, Wales

CHINA

Kunstindustrimuseet, Copenhagen, Denmark; Ethnographic Collection, Oslo University, Norway; Metropolitan Museum of Art, New York, USA; Philadelphia Museum of Art, Pennsylvania, USA; Victoria & Albert Museum, London; William Rockhill Nelson Gallery, Kansas City, Missouri, USA; Royal Ontario Museum, Toronto, Canada

FRANCE

Musée Carnavalet, Paris; Louvre, Paris; Musée des Arts Décoratifs, Paris; Musée Nissim de Camondo, Paris; Musée de Cluny, Paris; Musée de Malmaison, Paris; Musée Marmottan, Paris; Château de Versailles; Musée de Lyon; Bibliothèque Nationale, Paris; Château de Talcy; Musée de Strasbourg; Château de Champs, Paris; Chateau de Fontainebleau; Château de Chantilly; Château de Compiègne; Musée des Beaux-Arts, Tours; Bowes Museum, Barnard Castle. Co. Durham; Victoria & Albert Museum, London; Wallace Collection, London; Waddesdon Manor, Tring, Herts; Alnwick Castle, Northumberland; Luton Hoo (Wernher Collection), Luton, Bedfordshire; Rijksmuseum, Amsterdam, Holland; Residenzmuseum, Munich, Germany; Nationalmuseum, Stockholm, Sweden; Museum of Decorative Art, Oslo, Norway; Kunstindustrimuseet, Copenhagen, Denmark; Metropolitan Museum of Art, New York, USA; Frick Collection, New York, USA; Philadelphia Museum of Art, Pennsylvania, USA; Cleveland Museum of Art, Cleveland, Ohio, USA; Wadsworth Athenaeum, Hartford, Connecticut, USA; Montreal Museum of Fine Arts, Montreal, Canada; Musée de la Provence, Quebec City, Canada; Kunsthistorische Museum, Vienna, Austria; National Gallery of Art, Washington, DC., USA

GERMANY AND AUSTRIA

Staatliche Museum, Berlin; Bayaerisches Nationalmuseum, Munich; Germanisches Nationalmuseum, Nuremberg; Historisches Museum, Basel, Switzerland; Landesmuseum, Munster; Historisches Museum, Dresden; Landesmuseum Joanneum, Graz, Austria; Schweizerische Landesmuseum, Zurich, Switzerland; Museum für Kunst und Gewerbe, Hamburg; Museum für Kunsthandwerk, Frankfurt-am-Main; Stadtsmuseum, Cologne; Mainfrankisches Museum, Würzburg; Residenze, Bamberg; Residenz, Ansbach; Nordiska Museet, Stockholm, Sweden; Residenz, Wurzburg; Sanssouci, Potsdam; Museum für Kunsthandwerk, Dresden; Residenzmuseum, Munich; Schloss Schonbrunn, Vienna, Austria; Schloss

Pommersfelden, Bamberg; Schloss Charlottenburg, Berlin; Badisches Landesmuseum, Karlsruhe; Kunstgewerbemuseum, Berlin; Oesterreichisches Museum für Angewandte Kunst, Vienna, Austria; Kronberg Castle, Elsinore, Denmark; Kunstindustrimuseet, Copenhagen, Denmark; C.L. David Collection, Copenhagen, Denmark; Rijksmuseum, Amsterdam, Holland; Victoria & Albert, London

ISLAM

Tehran Museum, Iran; Victoria & Albert Museum, London; British Museum, London; Louvre, Paris; Metropolitan Museum of Art, New York, USA; Oriental Institute, Chicago, USA

ITALY

Palazzo Pitti, Florence; Museo Comunale Stibbert, Florence; Civici Instituti di Storia e d'Arte, Milan; Palazzo Rezzonico, Venice; Palazzo Reale, Genoa; Palazzo Reale, Turin; Palazzo del Quirinale, Rome; Hofburg, Vienna, Austria; Palais Czernin, Vienna, Austria; Palais Schwarzenburg, Vienna, Austria; Osterreichisches Barockmuseum, Vienna, Austria; Bundesmobiliendepot, Vienna, Austria; Palazzo Brignole, Genoa; Frick Collection, New York, USA; Palazzo Colonna, Rome; Palazzo Vecchio, Florence; Palazzo della Farnesina, Rome; Museo Horne, Florence; Palazzo Venezia, Rome; Museo Civico d'art Antica, Turin; Vatican Library, Rome; Museo del' Opificio della Pietre Dure, Florence; Wallace Collection, London; Fondazione Giorgio Cini, Venice; Metropolitan Museum of Art, New York, USA; Museo Civico Castello Sflorzesco, Milan; Museo Civico Correr, Venice; Kunstindustrimuseet, Copenhagen, Denmark; Rosenborg Collection, Copenhagen, Denmark

JAPAN

Kunstindustrimuseet, Copenhagen, Denmark; Honolulu Academy of Arts, Honolulu, Hawaii; Itsuo Art Museum, Ikeda, Osaka, Japan; Rosenborg Collection, Copenhagen, Denmark; Shoso-in Depot, Nara, Japan; National Museum, Tokyo, Japan; Victoria & Albert Museum, London; Ashmolean Museum, Oxford; City Art Gallery, Bristol; British Museum, London

LOW COUNTRIES

Rijksmuseum, Amsterdam, Holland; Musee Curtius, Liège, Belgium; Centraal Museum, Utrecht, Holland; Musées Royaux d'Art et d'Histoire, Brussels, Belgium; Kunstindustrimuseet, Copenhagen, Denmark; Metropolitan Museum of Art, New York, USA; Victoria & Albert Museum, London; Kronborg, Elsinore, Denmark

MEDIAEVAL EUROPE

Museo de Artes Decorativas, Madrid, Spain; Instituto de Valencia de don Juan, Madrid, Spain; Museo Nacional de Arte Antiga, Lisbon, Portugal; Victoria & Albert Museum, London; Kunstgewerbemuseum, Vienna, Austria; Louvre, Paris; Musée des Arts Decoratifs, Paris; Musée de Valère, Sion, Switzerland; Cathedral of Roda de Isabena, Huesca, Spain; Cathedral Museum, Halberstadt, Austria; Musée Carnavalet, Paris; Musée de Cluny, Paris; Stadtisches Museum, Wiesbaden, Germany; Bayerisches Nationalmuseum, Munich, Germany

POLAND

National Museum, Warsaw; Nieborow Palace, Poland; Rzeszow Museum, Poland

PORTUGAL AND PORTUGUESE COLONIES AND SPAIN AND SPANISH COLONIES

Museum of Art, Rhode Island School of Design, Providence, R.I., USA; Metropolitan Museum of Art, New York, USA; Hispanic Society of America, New York, USA; Brooklyn Museum, Latin America Gallery, New York, USA; Museum of New Mexico; Museo de Artes Decorativas, Barcelona, Spain; Museo de Artes Decorativas, Madrid, Spain; Fundacion Tavera-Lerma, Toledo, Spain; Municipal Museum, Portalegre, Portugal; Museu Soares dos Reis, Oporto, Portugal; Museu Nacional de Arte Antiga, Lisbon, Portugal; Palacio Nacional, Madrid, Spain; Museu Escola de Artes Decorativas, Lisbon, Portugal; Kunstindustrimuseet, Copenhagen, Denmark; Victoria & Albert Museum, London; National Museum, Stockholm, Sweden; Museu Guerra Junqueira, Oporto, Portugal; D. Celesta Cabral, Evora, Portugal; La Torre Lastres, Lima, Peru; Museo Historico Nacional, Buenos Aires, Argentina; Palacio Itamaraty, Rio de Janeiro, Brazil

PRE-COLUMBIAN AMERICA (NORTH AND SOUTH)

Instituto Nacional de Antropologia e Historia, Mexico City, Mexico; Archaeological Museum, Cuzco, Peru, South America; Brooklyn Museum, New York, USA; British Museum, London; Linden Museum, Stuttgart, Germany; Museum of the American Indian, New York; Museo de la Universidad Veracruzana, Mexico; American Museum of Natural History; Arizona State Museum, Tucson, Arizona, USA; Smithsonian Institution, Washington, DC., USA

ROME AND BYZANTIUM

Museo Capitolino, Rome; Kunstgewerbemuseum, Berlin; Louvre, Paris; Museo Nazionale, Naples, Italy; British Museum, London; Staatliche Museen, Berlin, Germany; Rijksmuseum, Kam, Nijmegen, Holland; Trier Museum, Germany

RUSSIA

State Historical Museum, Moscow; Nieborow Palace, Warsaw, Poland; Arkhangelskoe Palace, Moscow; Abramtsevo, Moscow; The State Hermitage Museum, St Petersburg; Victoria & Albert Museum, London; Catherine Palace, Tsarskoe Selo, St Petersburg; Winter Palace Museum, St Petersburg

SCANDINAVIA (DENMARK, NORWAY, SWEDEN)

Kronborg Castle, Elsinore, Denmark; Uppsala University, Uppsala, Sweden; Nordiska Museet, Stockholm, Sweden; Danish National History Museum, Fredericksborg Palace; Rosenberg Castle, Copenhagen, Denmark; National Museum, Stockholm, Sweden; Kunstindustrimuseet, Oslo, Norway; Fredensborg Palace, Denmark; Nationalmuseet, Copenhagen, Denmark; Kunstindustrimuseet, Copenhagen, Denmark; Historisk Museum, Bergen, Norway; Statens Historiska Museet, Stockholm, Sweden; Victoria & Albert Museum, London

USA

Brooklyn Museum, New York, USA; Wadsworth Athenaeum, Hartford, Connecticut; Henry du Pont Winterthur Museum, Winterthur, Delaware; Colonial Williamsburg, Virginia; Freer Gallery of Art, Washington, DC; Art Institute of Chicago, Chicago; Boston Museum of Fine Arts, Boston, Massachussetts; Metropolitan Museum of Art, New York; Cleveland Museum of Art, Cleveland, Ohio; Philadelphia Museum of Art, Philadelphia; Seattle Art Museum, Seattle, Washington; Museum of Art, Rhode Island School of Design, Providence, R.I.; Museum of City of New York; American Museum in Britain, Claverton, Bath; University of Yale Museum, Connecticut; Baltimore Museum of Art, Baltimore, Maryland; Henry Ford Museum, Dearborn, Michigan; New York Historical Society Collection, New York

Further Reading

GENERAL

Aronson, J. *The Encyclopaedia of Furniture*, London, 1970 edn.
Boger, L.A. *The Complete Guide to Furniture Styles*, London, 1961 edn.
Boger, L.A. & H.B. *The Dictionary of Antiques and the Decorative Arts*, New York, 1967 edn.
Hayward, H. (ed) *World Furniture*, London, 1969 edn.
Honour, H. *Cabinet-makers & Furniture designers*, London, 1969
Honour, H. *Chinoiserie*, London, 1961
Mercer, E. *Furniture: 700 to 1700*, London, 1969
Eames, P. *Furniture in England, France and the Netherlands from the 12th to the 15th centuries*, London, 1977
Thornton, P. *Seventeenth-century Interior Decoration in England, France and Holland*, London, 1978
Schmitz, H. (ed) *The Encyclopaedia of Furniture*, London, 1956 edn.
Wanscher, O. *The Art of Furniture*, trans. from Danish. London, 1968

AFRICA

African Furniture & Household Objects, American Federation of Arts, Indiana University Press, Bloomington, 1980.

ART NOUVEAU

Duncan, A. *Art Nouveau Furniture*, London, 1982

ANCIENT WORLD

Carcopino, J. *Daily Life in Ancient Rome*, London, 1956
Dunn, C.J. *Everyday Life in Traditional Japan*, London, 1969
Edwards, I.E.E. *The Pyramids of Egypt*, London, 1980 edn.
Liversidge, J. *Furniture in Roman Britain*, London, 1955
Loewe, M. *Everyday Life in Early Imperial China*, London, 1968
Rice, T.T. *Everyday Life in Byzantium*, London, 1967
Webster, T. *Everyday Life in Classical Athens*, London, 1969
White, J. Manchip, *Everyday Life in Ancient Egypt*, London, 1971
Saggs, H.W. *Everyday Life in Ancient Babylon & Assyria*, London, 1965

BRITAIN

Bly, J. *Discovering English Furniture*, Shire Books, 1988
Cescinsky, H. *English Furniture of the 18th Century*, 3 vols. London, 1911–12
Chinnery, V. *Oak Furniture: the British Tradition*, Woodbridge, 1990
Coleridge, A. *Chippendale Furniture*, London, 1968
Edwards, R. & Jourdain, M. *Georgian Cabinet-makers*, 3rd edn. London, 1955
Jackson, P. Ward. *English Furniture Designs of the 18th Century*, London, 1968
Joy, E. *Antique English Furniture*, London, 1972

Macquoid, P. & Edwards, R. *The Dictionary of English Furniture*, 2nd. edn. revised, 3 vols. London, 1954

EAST EUROPE AND RUSSIA

Chenevière, A. *Russian Furniture: the Golden Age, 1780–1840*, London, 1988
Maszkowska, B. *Z dziejów polskiego meblarstwa okresu oświecenia*, Warsaw, 1956
Cambridge Encyclopaedia of Russia, Cambridge, 1982

FRANCE

Packer, C. *Paris Furniture by the Master Ébénistes*, Monmouth, 1956
Souchal, G. *French 18th Century Furniture*, trans. London, 1961
Verlet, P. *French Royal Furniture*, trans. London, 1963
Verlet, P. *Les Meubles Français du XVIIIe siècle*, Paris, 1982
Verlet, P. *Le Style Louis XV*, Paris, 1942
Watson, F.J.B. *Louis XVI Furniture*, London, 1960

WESTERN EUROPE

Burr, G.H. *Hispanic Furniture*, New York, 1964
Henschen, I. & Blomberg, S. *Svenskt Mobellexikon*, Malmo, 1961
Lassen, E. *Danske Mobler, Denklassiske Periode*, Copenhagen, 1958
Pinto, A.C., *Cadeiras Portugueses*, Lisbon, 1952
Pluym, W. Van Der, *Vijf eeuwen binnenhuis en meubels in Nederland, 1450–1950*, Amsterdam, 1954
Schmitz, H. (ed). *Deutsche Mobel des Barock und Rokoko*. Stuttgart, 1923
Hunter, G.L. *Italian Furniture & Interiors*, London, 1920

AMERICA (inc. Pre-Columbian)

Bjerkoe, E. *Cabinet-makers of America*, New York, 1957
Bray, W. *Everyday Life of the Aztecs*, London, 1968
Burland, C.A. *Peoples of the Sun*, London, 1976
Davies, N. *The Ancient Kingdoms of Mexico*, London, 1983
Fagan, B. *Kingdoms of Gold, Kingdoms of Jade*, London

FACSIMS OF EARLIER PATTERN BOOKS

Chippendale, Thomas. *The Gentleman & Cabinet-maker's Director*, 1966
Hepplewhite, George. *The Cabinet-maker & Upholsterer's Guide*, 1969
Hope, Thomas. *Household Furniture and Interior Decoration*, 1971
Ince, W. & Mayhew, J. *The Universal System of Household Furniture*, 1960
Sheraton, Thomas. *The Cabinet-maker and Upholsterer's Drawing Book*, 1971
Smith, George. *Collection of Designs for Household Furniture*, 1970

JOURNALS

Furniture History: Journal of the Furniture History Society, 1965–
Connoisseur, Country Life, Antique Collector, Apollo, Burlington Magazine, Collector's Guide.

GLOSSARY

arabesques: type of ornament for borders or panels, composed of naturalistic elements, foliate and figural, loosely derived from Moorish ornament.

arcading: ornamental decoration in the form of a series of arches supported on columns or pilasters.

armoire: French word for wardrobe, an upright cupboard with two doors, usually between about 5 ft. and 8 ft. tall.

auricular decoration: a form of decoration in which parts of the body (bones, flesh, muscle) are used, giving an overall effect of the curves of the human ear: this was popular in W. Europe in 17th cent. (Drawing on page 72.)

backstool: 'a low stool with a back thereto' (1588 definition): a stool with a simple, usually single, stile added at the back to make a chair. Upright chairs were known as backstools throughout the 17th cent.

baluster: turned shape on legs or columns, usually bulbous like a vase.

banding: ornamental border of a furniture surface made of a colour, grain or type of wood different from the wood of the surface.

Baroque: probably from the Spanish *barucca* meaning deformed pear, the term describes the architectural and decorative style of the late 16th and much of the 17th cent. (and even into the 18th cent.) which is characterized by rich decorative effects, using rounded contours, much foliage, contrasting colours, sculptured forms and so forth. It originated in Italy and followed the Mannerist form of Renaissance.

bergère **chair:** French term for upholstered wing armchair (supplied with a cushion), introduced sometime in the 18th cent. (drawing on page 63).

boarded construction: construction of furniture, especially chests, tables, stools, using boards fixed together with nails, sometimes reinforced on corners with metal brackets. Boarding was succeeded by joined construction (see **dovetailing, mortice and tenon**).

bobbin turning: a style of wood turning for legs, stretchers and stiles, in which the turned wood resembled a bobbin or a line of bobbins.

bombé: French term for swelling out of fronts and also sides of carcase furniture, especially *commodes* (see colour section).

bonheur-du-jour: French term for type of small writing table on legs, sometimes with a section at the back containing drawers, shelves, etc. Introduced mainly for women's use in the mid-18th cent. and popular up to the Revolution, (drawing on page 61).

bowfronted: convex fronting to furniture, notably in mid- and late 18th cent. including chests of drawers, sideboards, corner cupboards.

breakfront: term describing the construction of a piece of carcase furniture in which the central portion projects in front of the remainder of the piece.

buffet: This term is applied to so many pieces of furniture, and not all of the same kind, that there is much to be said for dropping it out altogether from furniture nomenclature, as it is in this book.

bureau: French word for desk (and also for study, office, department, board). In French, its desk connotation means either a desk with a slope top (*bureau à pente*) or a writing table with drawers either side of a knee-hole, or a writing table with a single row of drawers under the top (*bureau plat*). In English, it has come to mean a writing desk consisting of short and long drawers surmounted by a section with pigeon holes and small drawers, a covered 'well' for storage, the whole enclosed by a sloping front which when lowered to horizontal forms a writing surface. If it has a bookcase on top, it is called a *bureau* bookcase, but this is not to be confused with a *secrétaire* bookcase (q.v.).

bureau **bookcase:** see *bureau* (above)

cabriole leg: type of leg that curves outwards on the downward path and then curves inwards, tapering at the same time, and ending in a decorative foot. Fitted to chairs, stools, tables, stands, and occasionally as foot to cupboards, cabinets, chests. The style originated in China, and became popular in Europe at the end of the 17th cent. and for decades in the 18th cent. The knee of the cabriole leg is sometimes carved.

canted corner: cut or angled corner of a rectilinear surface, such as on chests, cupboards. Also known as bevelled or chamfered.

***caquetoire* (or *caqueteuse*):** a later 16th cent. chair with a high, narrow back and widely splayed arms. The seat was usually trapezoid in plan. Intended for women to sit on while chatting (French: *caqueter* = to gossip). Made in Britain, France, and the Low Countries, (drawing on page 79).

carcase: the body of a piece of case furniture, that is, chest, cupboard, *bureau*, cabinet, etc. on which veneers of wood are glued for surface decoration, or which are lacquered or painted.

cartonnier: French term for a piece of ancillary furniture made to hold papers, and usually fitted to or rested upon the back or one side of a writing table.

cartouche: decorative tablet featuring scrollwork or other curled ornament, made of wood or gilt-bronze or silver, on which is sometimes engraved a motif such as a coat of arms.

caryatid: sculptured figure of a woman used as a support on a piece of furniture or as decorative moulding.

cassapanca: Italian term for a chest made with a raised back to form a seat.

cassone: Italian word for chest, in particular the highly carved and ornamented Renaissance style variety, of which great numbers were made.

chinoiserie: decorative artwork that has Chinese motifs, such as pagodas, fretwork, figures of Chinese men and women, trees, etc. as conceived in Western terms.

claw and ball foot: usually at the end of a cabriole leg, it represents a bird's talons (or a dragon's claw) clutching a sphere.

chevron: a zig-zag pattern of moulded wood or of inlay work.

club, or pad, foot: simple end to a cabriole leg, resembling the pad of an animal foot.

clustered column: a style of table or chair leg made up from a number of pillars clustered together (drawing on page 75).

commode: French word for chest of drawers, and in France usually confined to pieces with two or three long drawers. The *commode à l'anglaise* had a set of open shelves at each end beyond the main chest of drawers part. The *commode à encoignures* was much the same kind of piece, but the shelves were enclosed with doors. Where the drawers of a *commode* are enclosed behind a pair of doors, the *commode* is often called a *commode à vantaux.*

confidante: an upholstered settee with extra seats at each end beyond the arms and set at an angle: its counterpart, the *indiscret,* was arranged as three linked armchairs (drawing on page 67).

console table: a side table resting on one or two legs at the front, but which has to be fixed to the wall at the back for support. In the 18th cent. these were elaborately decorated, and often surmounted with colourful marble tops.

contador: Portuguese cabinet with several rows of drawers, usually set on a separate and elaborately decorated stand.

cornice: the horizontal moulded top of a piece of cabinet furniture, which projects forwards and out sideways, such as on a bureau bookcase or a chest-on-chest.

court cup-board (or court cup-board): see cup-board.

cresting rail: the shaped and sometimes also pierced ornament on the top of a chair-back. Usually, the two upright stiles and the centre splat slot into the rail and are glued in place. A great variety of designs of cresting rail have emerged over the centuries.

cross-banding: banding of wood whose grain is generally set at right angles to the direction of the grain of the principal wood surface and often in different wood from that of the surface.

cup-board: This was a mediaeval term for a side table of one, two or three tiers, for displaying plate and food, or for serving from during meals (a board for cups), i.e. an open table. Later, it came to be called a court cup-board, from the French word *court*=short, probably because it was lower than eye level in height. In the 16th cent. some of these court cup-boards began to acquire hinged doors between the top and middle tiers, creating enclosures for storage. These came to be known as court cupboards (because by that time a cupboard was an alternative term for an aumbry, or wardrobe). They also came to be called press cupboards if both (or three) stages were enclosed by doors. When court or press cupboards were used for storing food and drink, and some of the utensils and vessels with which to consume them, they would often be referred to as livery cupboards, although there is still controversy over the exact definition of a livery cupboard.

cwpwrdd deudarn and ***cwpwrdd tridarn:*** Welsh versions of the two-stage and three-stage court (or press) cup-board or cupboard (see cup-board). The Welsh versions usually have the bottom stage enclosed by a pair or three doors.

cylinder-top desk: desk whose working area is enclosed by a quarter cylinder of wood that moves upwards and downwards to open and close it. The up movement puts the cylinder into the desk carcase. If the cylinder is made of connected slats of wood arranged in an arc, it is often called a roll-top desk. In French, the term *bureau à cylindre* covers desks with either roll top or cylinder top.

dovetailing: method of joining end grain into side grain at right angles, such as in drawer corners, by cutting and fitting shaped projections into corresponding cuts. First devised in the later 16th cent. it became a standard form of drawer and carcase jointing from the early 17th.

dressoir: French term for a piece of late mediaeval furniture of two or three stages. The top stage was an open shelf with a carved back panel, under which was a second stage enclosed by carved doors flanking a centre panel and, sometimes, below that another open shelf at the bottom. Sometimes the lower shelf was enclosed with doors and panel. The profile of *dressoirs* was semi-hexagonal or rectangular.

ébéniste: French term for cabinet-maker specializing in veneered furniture, as distinct from *menuisier* (q.v.). The term comes from ebony (ébène), one of the first woods for veneering in France.

encoignure: French word for corner cupboard.

escutcheon: bronze or brass or silver plate, usually decorated in some way, placed over a keyhole in a drawer or door.

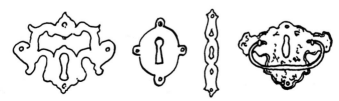

fauteuil: French word for armchair. There were several kinds, especially in the 18th cent., and among them were the *fauteuil en bergère* (see *bergère*) the *fauteuil de cabinet* (desk chair) and the *fauteuil à la Reine* which had a flat back (drawing on p. 58).

feather-banding: a decorative veneer of two narrow strips of veneer laid side by side diagonally, to form a pattern resembling a herring-bone or feather, contrasting with the surface veneer beside which it is laid. Used mostly on drawer fronts, table tops, bureau fall-fronts, it is also called herring-bone inlay.

figuring: using the natural pattern of wood in veneered form to enhance the texture of wood, usually by a variety of patterns, particularly with walnut, mahogany, yew, elm, mulberry and laburnum.

fluting: decoration in which concave grooves are cut into wood in rows close together, or separated by flat strips or convex reeding.

fretwork: wood carving in patterns of straight lines, open or as raised moulding on surfaces. This is a feature of Chinese taste.

frieze: band of decorated wood below a cornice (q.v.). It can be decorated with carving or brass inlay, or fretwork.

gateleg table: oval, round, square, rectangular or otherwise shaped, with hinged leaves held horizontal by swing-out gate-like supports.

gesso: Form of carved relief decoration. The motif is carved or modelled in a mix of size and plaster or whiting, and then surfaced with gold leaf or gold paint imitation, when it is often called gesso gilt.

gilt bronze: otherwise known as *ormolu*. Cast and gilded bronze or brass, used for mounts and other applied decoration on furniture.

grille: lattice or trellis work of brass as filling for cabinet furniture doors or galleries.

grotesque: decorative sculpture on wood with fantastic interweaving of human and animal forms, sometimes with foliage, urns, anthemium, etc. so named from *grotti*, or walls in Roman ruins on which such designs were found.

hoof foot: end of a cabriole leg resembling an animal (often goat's) hoof.

inlay: surface decoration made by insetting separate pieces of woods of differing colours, or other materials such as stone, ivory, mother-of-pearl, bone, metal, etc. in recessed ground.

intarsia: Italian word for inlay or marquetry. (see also page 42).

lacquer: the process of applying several layers of paint and special varnish to produce a decorated surface.

linenfold: a type of wood-carving representing folded linen. It was used in Gothic and early Renaissance furniture, especially on Flemish and English panelling.

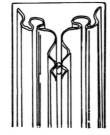

livery cupboard: see cup-board

lozenge: ornament in diamond pattern, carved or inlaid.

marquetry: inlay work of veneers of wood of different colours and grains in delicate patterns.

menuisier: French term for wood craftsman who makes solid wood furniture such as beds, chairs and other things of plain or carved wood.

mortise and tenon: main form of joining wood members. The end of one member has a rectangular slot (mortise) into which a similar dimension rectangular recessed projection (tenon) fits. The two are glued, sometimes assisted by means of dowels right through the join.

moulding: shaped member to ornament cornices, plinths, panel frames, etc. In some pieces, mouldings were shaped separately and then applied to a piece.

gadrooning

egg and tongue

knulling

pear drop

guilloche

key pattern

egg and dart

lunette

mount: gilt bronze, bronze or brass, and occasionally silver, sculptured fitting for corners, edges and surfaces of furniture, for decoration.

mudéjar: a distinctive Hispano-Moorish style of architecture and furniture of the late 15th and early to mid 16th cent. in Spain (drawing on page 85).

neo-classical: style of architecture, decoration and furniture that began in France and Britain in the 1760s as a result of growth in knowledge of Greek and Roman forms, and as a reaction against Rococo style.

ormolu: see gilt bronze.

oyster veneer: type of veneer where the wood is cut from small branches and laid together to form a pattern resembling a group of oysters lying next to each other. Used particularly on cabinet surfaces, chests, long-case clocks, and popular in the later 17th cent. and early 18th cent. The principal woods were laburnum, olive, walnut.

parquetry: wood inlay pattern made up from wood of same colour but different grain. The patterns are usually geometric.

patera: round or oval ornament in flat form but carrying low relief decoration.

pediment: triangular structure on the top of certain items of furniture, such as some cabinets, bookcases, long-case clocks, etc.

Pembroke table: small table with short drop leaves held up by swinging-out wood brackets. The term was first used by Chippendale, and is said to derive from a Lady Pembroke who ordered a table from his firm.

pietre dure: Italian term for a hard stone ornamental decoration of table tops, decorative cabinets, etc. It was introduced in Florence in the 15th cent.

pilaster: rectangular column attached to a piece of furniture, such as the front corners of a chest of drawers.

press cupboard: a modification of a court cupboard (see cupboard), in which there were enclosed cupboards in top and bottom stages.

quartering: means of producing a formal pattern in wood veneer by setting four consecutively cut pieces of veneer with the same figuring in opposing senses to give a mirrored effect. Popular between *c.*1670–*c.*1740, on table tops, chests, cupboard doors, and some bureau slope fronts.

rail: horizontal part of a joined frame of a piece of furniture, or across a chair seat at back, front or sides.

reeding: form of wood decoration of rows of adjacent convex mouldings, as surfacing for a turned leg or as ornament on flat surfaces.

Régence: strictly, the period 1715–1723 when Philippe d'Orléans acted as Regent of France in the minority of Louis XV (1715–74), but in furniture covering the changing style between Louis XIV and Louis XV, and lasting roughly from 1710 to 1735.

ribbonwork: decoration in wood or plaster in the form of ribbons and bows.

Rococo: *Rocaille* was the French word to describe a style of decorative art first evolved in France in *c.*1700, largely by Jean Bérain (see page 52). The style was called Rococo in most parts of Europe later on, and is characterized by shell and rock decorative forms, with foliage, flowers, scrolls, tortuous curves, with emphasis on asymmetry, and often described as a gay and irresponsible style. It was a reaction against more formal Baroque forms.

Romayne work: Renaissance style of carving heads in roundels or on square panels, the heads sometimes being portraits of living or dead personalities. 16th cent.

sabre leg: a chair leg with a concave curve, originating from ancient Hittite and Greek designs. Popular in Western Europe, especially Britain, from about 1800.

secrétaire: French word for a cabinet enclosed by a fall or drop front, the front when horizontal being used as a writing surface. In these instances it is usually called a *secrétaire à abattant*. Other types of *secrétaire* include a *secrétaire en pente* which was a lean-to desk with a flat slope top that could be locked in place over the drawers and pigeon holes (this piece was superseded by the cylinder-top desk.

secretaire bookcase: a two-stage piece consisting of a top cupboard half with shelves and enclosed by glazed (or more rarely) solid doors, on a chest of drawers whose top drawer has a fall-front behind which is a writing surface and rows of small drawers and pigeon-holes. The lower drawers are long drawers. An alternative arrangement beneath the fall-front covered desk drawer is a cupboard enclosing shelves.

secretary: modern American term for a desk enclosed by a sloping front, with a cabinet on top and drawers underneath. Not the same as the French *secrétaire* (q.v.).

shield-back: chair-back popularized though not invented by Hepplewhite, where the uprights and cresting rail are carved and joined to form a shield-shaped outline, in which is fitted a central carved and pierced splat.

spandrel: the space between the curve of an arch and the frame in which it is contained, or the decorated triangle or segment inserted in that space.

splat: upright panel or wood slotted between the back seat rail and the cresting rail on top of a chair, in solid or pierced and decorated form.

stile: vertical member of framework at the end or corner of a piece of panelled furniture, or of a chair-back.

strapwork: ornament carved in low relief, often in repetitive design, suggesting interlaced metal ornament, sometimes mixed with foliage, flowers, etc.

stretcher: horizontal rail or bar with varying forms of decorative treatment, or alternatively plain, joining legs of chairs or tables, at high, middle or low level, for strengthening the structure.

stringing: line or lines of inlay (wood or metal) used as decorative border or dividing lines between areas of veneer or solid wood surfaces.

swag: festoon of fruit, flowers, nuts, leaves, as decorative motif, carved or painted, on furniture.

swash turning: otherwise called barley-sugar twist turning, this is a form of wood-turning especially popular in later 17th cent. furniture, particularly for stretchers, stiles or legs of chairs or tables.

scagliola: see page 45.

split baluster: an ornament of turned baluster design where the turned piece is split longitudinally and one half applied as ornament to furniture.

tambour front: a curved sliding top to a writing desk well, or front to a cupboard, where thin, convex mouldings are glued side by side on their flat surfaces on to strong canvas, the ends slotting into grooves so as to form a sliding shutter.

tester: from the French '*tête*' = head, a wood canopy over a bed which has two or four corner posts. If it covers only the top half of the bed, it is called a half-tester.

turning: method of producing legs, pillars, uprights, etc. on

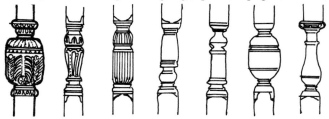

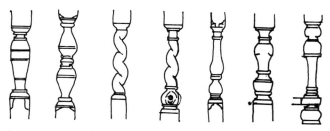

furniture in rounded form. Wood was turned on a pole lathe, until the advent of machine turning in the early 19th cent.

veneer: thin layer of wood, originally cut by hand, but by machine after *c.*1810, used to decorate wholly or partially the carcase of a piece of furniture.

volute: a spiral type scroll, characteristic of classical capitals in architecture, applied to furniture decoration.

INDEX

PHOTOGRAPHIC ACKNOWLEDGEMENTS

Ipswich Borough Council Museums and Galleries: Colour section pages 2 (bottom), 4 (bottom), 5 (bottom), 6 (top and bottom), 7 (top and bottom), 8 (top).

By courtesy of the Board of Trustees of the Victoria & Albert Museum: Page 1 (top).